IASGACH AN ALBA

FISHING SCOTLAND
a guide to game fishing
ROSS & CROMARTY
SUTHERLAND & CAITHNESS

D1407517

Cover design and illustrations by Robin Kyle

R. Kyle 95

© James Coutts 1998

By the same author:
Game Fishing Guide to Inverness-shire 1967
Game Fishing Guide to Argyllshire 1967
Game Fishing Guide to Shetland 1968
Game Fishing Guide to Orkney 1968
Game Fishing Guide to the Outer Hebrides 1969
Game Fishing Guide to Sutherland & Caithness 1969
Game Fishing Guide to Inverness-shire, Skye, Moray & Nairn 1995
Game Fishing Guide to Inverness-shire, Skye, Moray & Nairn 1996
Game Fishing Guide to Argyll and Islands and Loch Lomond 1996
Game Fishing in Ross & Cromarty, Sutherland & Caithness 1996
Game Fishing in Inverness-shire, Skye, Moray & Nairn 1997
Game Fishing in Ross & Cromarty, Sutherland & Caithness 1997
Game fishing in Argyll, the Isles, Loch Lomond, Stirling & Trossachs 97
Game Fishing in Inverness-shire, Skye, Moray & Nairn 1998
Game fishing in Argyll, the Isles, Loch Lomond, Stirling & Trossachs 98

A record of this book is available from the British Library
ISBN: 1 900417 08 1

Published by Fishing Scotland
Printed by Nevisprint, Fort William
Cover art and illustrations by:
Robin Kyle 10 Seafield Gardens Fort William PH33 6RJ

While every effort is made to ensure information and charges detailed are current, no
responsibility is accepted for change, alteration, cancellation or non availability of
fishing, permit or services implied or considered in this book.

Providers of private, hotel, club, association, and commercial fisheries and services
generally available by permit are encouraged to provide details for consideration of
inclusion in future editions:

**FISHING SCOTLAND Roy Bridge Inverness-shire PH31 4AG
Scotland
Tel/Fax: (01397) 712 812**
www.fishing-scotland.co.uk email:info@fishing-scotland.co.uk

Preface

You will find I have recorded in this guide a fair assessment and expectations with due consideration to the vagarities of the fishing game. Not all waters where one can enjoy a few casts are here recorded. Many lochs, lochans and streams can be fished simply by making a mannerly request to the owner or keeper. These waters, I leave to be found by initiative. However, do please ask first.

Regarding access in the Highlands, ask locally what the current situation is before you venture into open country. In wild and remote regions it is easy to dismiss as of no consequence ones presence on the hill. Shooting, lambing, and other hill work are important to the success of the seasons work and can on occasions require that others do not access certain areas prepared for that work. Responsible fishers, hillwalkers, ornithologists, or just walk about the country kind of people have interest and respect for those who work in such wild places and always ask permission before going on the hill.

Another subject of vital importance to be considered, is the misconception that the burns, rivers and lochs of the Highlands can continue to provide the fish, our wee broon troot no less, together with salmon, sea trout, ferox and char without research, prepared planning and good management. There are too many fishers now for nature to balance the taking without assistance in conservation. To sustain and continue to provide sport fishing has a price, with modest cost to the angler. Protection orders are here to stay, with the letter of their intention followed, fishings should be sustained and many cases improved. The newly formed Trusts of Sutherland, and Lochaber with intended cooperative resource and research will require the support of every fisher, club, and association if they are to succeed.

To all who shared with me, their experience, knowledge or maybe just a nod or a wave by loch or river, thank you.

Bill Rogey Brown M B E who kindly created the forward, reflects the very heart beat of Highland fishing. This wee book will be that much greater value to the reader who implements like attitude and consideration. Thank you, Bill.

Aye
James Coutts
Roy Bridge, Lochaber
March 1998.

FORWARD

Angling for game fish in the Highlands of Scotland must be one of the most pleasurable and relaxing recreations one can imagine. During my life I have had so many happy years with rod and line pursuing my sport and I have many memories to fall back upon during times of illness and immobility. Fishing for salmon, sea trout and brown trout have given me so much satisfaction and excitement. To be able to express what I feel about angling in printed word gives me the ultimate enjoyment especially if the reader reciprocates.

However, when as a young man I caught my first grilse in the fifties, migratory fish were plentiful and looking back it seemed so easy to go out on a loch or river, after work, and catch the fish of my choice. These were great times, But it did not last.

Why? First the scientists discovered where the young salmon went to feed, the result - overfishing. Then in the late sixties UDN (Ulcerative Dermal Necrosis) spread to the UK from Ireland and that seemed disastrous, and so it was at the time. Thankfully it did not last too long. Then came the salmon fish farming industry with its cages sited in our west coast sea lochs. Consequently, the salmon cages attracted a tremendous increase in the sea lice population which infested the sea trout and caused heavy mortality wiping out much of the stock.

Depressing, isn't it! All is not lost, however. Many organisations such as the North Atlantic Salmon Conservation Organisation, the Atlantic Salmon Trust, the North Atlantic Salmon Fund, the Scottish Office, the Scottish Rivers Boards, the newly created Fishery Trusts and many other angling organisations set to and undertook conservation measures to stop the rot and help in restoration of our migratory fish.

Already, following the moving of salmon farm cages away from the immediate vicinity of sea trout river estuaries the sea trout stocks in the west coast of Scotland have dramatically increased. Catches on Loch Maree increased 400% in 1996 and Loch Hope increased catch returns by 100% in 96' over 1995. So one way or another conservation measures are working.

James Coutts, author of this guide, for whom I have a great deal of respect, and I, are dedicated to the conservation and development of game fish and it is a privilege to be asked to contribute to the forward of this guide.

We are so lucky here in Scotland, think of the disasters that befell Canada and the USA last century where great rivers like those in New England were ruined by the industrial revolution and are void of Atlantic salmon. Not a thought was spared for future generations.

Here in Scotland we do our best to preserve our heritage, and are winning.

Good luck and tight lines,

Bill Rogie Brown M B E

CONTENTS

XX A THREAT TO SALMON – SEE PAGE 63XX

SAFETY CONSIDERATIONS

Fishing like other water oriented recreations or pastimes requires continual awareness of the hazards of being in, on or close to that environment. The consequences of an error of judgement, accident or the thoughtlessness of others **may well result in drowning.**

Whether you can swim or not, a properly fitting life jacket or buoyancy aid should be worn on your person while in any small boat or close to water.

Alcohol contributes to more boating accidents than all other causes.

Standing up or moving about within a boat is the major cause of man overboard and capsize accidents.

Overloading is a common cause of accidents.

COLD CAN KILL - IF IN DOUBT! DO NOT GO OUT

THE LAW WHILE FISHING IN SCOTLAND

The following is intended to ensure the reader will be aware of likely instances of law infringement or where confrontation may occur.

It is an offence for any person to fish for or take salmon or sea trout without written permission.

It is prohibited throughout Scotland to fish for or take salmon or sea trout on a Sunday.

A fishing permit covers one rod only, unless otherwise specified.

Fishing rods (except in sea or course fishing) must be hand held. Rod/s set up on river bank or loch shores are set lines and illegal in Scotland.

The open season to fish for brown trout is from 15th March through 6th October. Frequently, this period is lawfully curtailed.

A **Protection Order** in effect, is the instrument of protection of an area of water under management to improve viable fishing. It is an offence to fish a protected water without a current permit on your person. The permit charge on such waters is used directly to effect and improve and possibly develop that water **for the rod and line angler.**

Private property access is NOT open to any person who does not have the permission of the owner/s.

A mannerly request or inquiry may well avoid a confrontation.

If in any doubt! Check locally - before fishing.

PART ONE
ROSS & CROMARTY

Stretching from the east to west coasts and covering 2,000 square miles Ross and Cromarty can cause visitors some astonishment to find such diversity of natural beauty in one area. From the rich rolling pastures of the Black Isle and Easter Ross through the stark and enigmatic central moorland to the grandeur and spectacle of the west coast. Fast flowing rivers, secluded bays, the meandering firths, gentle hills , breathtaking mountains, glorious lochs of every shape and size, tiny villages, bustling towns - Ross and Cromarty has a distinctive character all of its own. Entering Ross and Cromarty by the Kessock bridge you look down on the charming villages of North Kessock and Kilmuir, both on the shore of the firth. By the roadside just off the bridge, with lovely views up the firth towards the mountainous west is the **North Kessock Tourist Information Centre (01463) 731 505** where enthusiastic and knowledgeable staff are primed and ready to welcome and advise on everything from accommodation to pony trekking, trout fishing and ancient monuments. West at the head of the Cromarty Firth lies Dingwall the bustling administrative and market centre of Ross and Cromarty. To the west rugged mountains form a barrier to the seaboard which is negotiated by excellent roads where the scenic grandeur will impress the most seasoned of travellers. So it is, on through the pass to Achnasheen and beyond where the legendary Loch Maree draws fishers in search of mighty sea trout. Torridon remote and beautiful with as much water in sight as mountain and glen of which Queen Victoria wrote of her visit of 1877 **"The grand, wild, savage looking, but most beautiful and picturesque Glen of Torridon opened upon us, with the dark mural precipices of that extraordinary mountain Ben Liathach"** just as dramatic today, you come and see! Continue north by Gairloch, Poolewe, Aultbea, Laide and Gruinard to Braemore and so to Ullapool and the isolated Achiltibuie headland where nature is still not bounded by man, where wild cat, red deer, pine martin, kestrel, buzzard, and eagle are likely encounters if you take the time. Rich in heritage many Ross and Cromarty place names originate in Norse occupation of 800 years ago - Diabaig (Deep Bay); Shieldaig (Herring Bay); Ardheslaig (Hazel Bay). Applecross should not be missed, One of the earliest seats of Christianity in Scotland with Iona retains an aura of calm tranquillity. A great place for family holidays.

EASTER ROSS AND CROMARTY
RIVER CONON and TRIBUTARIES

The Conon, which enters the Cromarty Firth near the town of Dingwall is part of the largest river system in the county. The main tributaries are the Rivers Blackwater, Bran, Meig and Orrin and numerous lochs including Achonachie, Meig, Scardroy, Achanalt, Chuilinn, Garve and Luichart some of which were created by one or other of the nine dams built to harness hydro electric power. From the estuary upstream good stretches are available for salmon, sea trout and brown trout fishing by day or weekly permit.

LOCH ACHONACHIE ANGLING CLUB WATERS

There is no substitute for experience and it really shows with this club which provides excellent maps and details of regulations with day permits. The salmon and trout waters owned or controlled by the club are all well maintained in bank or shore access with visitors welcome and encouraged. There is **No Fishing on Sundays** on any club waters. **Permits are available only from: The Village Shop & Post Office at Marybank village on the A832.**

UPPER RIVER CONON 4 Beats - 3 rods per beat

Session charges:	dawn to 4pm	5pm to dusk
April/May	£5	£5
June/July	£10	£7
Aug/Sept	£15	£8

Outboard motor and fuel £8 per day - Life jackets £2 per day

Salmon and Brown trout   **Season 1 April - 30 September**

From its junction with River Meig to its entry at the west end of loch Achonachie the River Conon has 9 named fishing pools and a considerable amount of unnamed water which is worth attention. This is **fly only** water with the exception that spinning is permitted when Loch Luichart power station is generating. Low water compensation flow provides excellent fly conditions in surroundings of great scenic beauty and rural environment. There are casting platforms at all the right places with bank maintenance reflecting long-standing experienced management. Brown trout on this section are well above the average Highland river at a true 12oz with a few 3 to 4 lbs taken each season. Salmon fly patterns are **Blue Charm, Hairy Mary, Stoats Tail, Munro Killer and Ally's Shrimp** in sizes **8 to 12**. For trout, **Black Pennel, Grouse and Claret, Blae and Black and Dark Mackerel** in size **12/14** are sure fire attractors.

UPPER RIVER BLACKWATER
Season: Brown Trout 1 April - Salmon 1 June - 30 September
Both Banks - 8 rods - Sessions/Charges as Upper River Conon

The grand Highland atmosphere of this location with ease of access to such wonderful surroundings is perhaps one of the reasons so many return here year after year. That the Salmon returns have improved to equal and frequently better the Upper Conon and the brown trout are truly of a recorded 13 oz average could have been one of the best kept secrets of club. The fish pass at Rogie Falls is not opened until 1 April hence the late start with the waiting fish streaking right through to Loch na Croic with the result that it is June through August that produces newly arrived residents which give the best sport. There are 15 good pools from the outflow of Loch na Croic to just above the Rogie Falls with more than enough room for the rods permitted. Fly fishing is the order of things with restricted spinning. Trout fishing really is excellent with a high average that draws the keen trout fly fisher. This is certainly a water that is close to ideal for the angler who comes prepared to fish for salmon or trout. Wee flees as for the Conon will get you some real crash takes.

LOCH ACHONACHIE
Salmon and Brown Trout   Season: 1 April - 30 September
Charges: Bank £4.00 per rod day - £10.00 per week
Boats £10.00 dawn to 4pm - £6.00 5pm to dusk

The River Conon flows in the west end and out of the east end of this loch with all migratory fish passing in the opposite direction towards the headwaters. Access is very easy the Strathconon road never far from the south bank. In particular, the trout are of excellent quality with recorded catches over the last few season showing a 12/13oz average. Spinning or trolling is permitted and fish are taken from throughout the length and breadth of the loch. Early salmon move right through and it is mid July through September that most are taken.

LOCH MEIG - FLY ONLY - Charges as Loch Achonachie
Brown Trout   Season: 1 April - 30 September

Bank and boat fishing are permitted on this fine fly only loch which lies in Strathconon surrounded by 2000 ft plus mountains so presenting the feeling that you might be in wilderness far from the summer

3

crowds. The road is close to the lochs south shore and allows very easy access. Fishing for or taking salmon is prohibited at all times. Regulations set a bag limit of 10 trout per boat or 5 per rod per session which is as it should be for the sports angler. Brown trout here are a wee bit heavier than most averages with 1lb being confirmed from records which is a good enough reason for getting up here any time from the end of April when spring is beginning to warm things up just a mite. Locally June and July are best favoured though so long as a westerly creates a bit of chop fine fishing will prevail through August and September. There are 3 boats on the loch and these are very popular so advance booking is a good idea. The usual Scottish loch flies from 10 to 12 under normal conditions apply but if its honking with whitecaps try an **8 Black Spider on the bob and an 8 Dark Mackerel in the middle and a 10 Heather Moth on the tail**. You will have great fun.

LOCH SCARDROY - Permits as Loch Achonachie

A great location at the head of Strathconon this is just the place for a family picnic and for learner fly fishers for there is an excellent head of fine wee troot of 3 to the pound who would just love to take you on. As with fishin' and life in general some things make the world run that bit easier and its a warm west wind that provides the expected basket of wee fat trout for breakfast! There are 2 boats available here and Spinning is permitted.

Club permits are available and boats can be prebooked only from: The Village Shop & Post Office, Marybank (01997) 433201 where club motors are issued and all manner of daily supplies are available at this licensed store. Permit sales 8-6pm Mon-Fri, 8-5pm Saturday, no fishing on Sunday, so no permit issue.

RIVER BLACKWATER - INCHBAE LODGE HOTEL

Nestling on the banks of the Blackwater just six miles west of Garve on the A835 Patrick and Judy Price the resident owners offers free wild brown trout fishing on the Blackwater to resident guests and are able to arrange hill loch trouting and salmon fishing. (01997) 455269

DINGWALL & DISTRICT ANGLING CLUB

This clubs exceptional waters produce about 60 salmon and in excess of 600 sea trout and finnock annually. **Sports & Model Shop 66 High Street Dingwall Tel: (01349) 862 346** Issues visitor permits Monday through Friday only. £10.00 per day till 1 June - £15 thereafter.

RIVER CONON - FLY ONLY

Sea Trout and Salmon   Season: 26 January - 30 September

The extent of available fishing is tidal. As such, together with the probability of hydro generation run off and rapid rise in water level care and vigilance is a priority of fishing here with the use of chest waders prohibited throughout. The majority of anglers come here to fish for sea trout and are given every assistance with a good map being supplied with daily permits which diagrams the various pools of which there are 9 reliable holding stretches from the railway bridge at Conon Bridge on the A862, downstream to the estuary. As with most tidal waters, from just prior to high tide and following the ebb is professed to be the most productive. The odd sea trout can be expected from opening day with some little concentration of finnock occurring through March building to significant catches in May through July by which time sea trout are also in good numbers. Only bank fishing is permitted with access such that one can easily move downstream with the ebb to New Pool at the bottom. July and August are the most productive period for salmon. Sea trout flies locally favoured are **Teal Blue and Silver, Peter Ross, Greenwells, and Dunkeld in size 12/14.**

LOCHS ACHANALT & CHUILINN

Brown Trout, Pike and Perch   Season 15 March - 6 October

Fishing of these easy to reach roadside lochs was offered by the club at no charge until very recently. This welcome invitation to the casual angler, local or visitor may well change in the near future. No reflection on the club, local estates appear to be considering some sort of development! Make inquiry locally for 97'. Located on the left of A832 just west of where that road branches off the A835 after passing through Garve. All legal methods have been the order of things with three to the pound brownies the prize. This is an excellent place to take kids for a picnic or learners such is the freedom from obstructions and the enthusiasm of the wee broon troot. Scenery is wonderful, rugged and Highland without the requirement of a cross country march.

GLEN ORRIN FISHERY - LOCH KELPIE - fly only
Rainbow, Brown Trout and Orrin Blues - Open all year

This small put and take is located on the property of a fish farm with hyper active stock in best condition. Home of the Orrin Blue hybrid, which will fool you with both the spunk and looks of a Punk rocker sea trout this unique blue flash is the product of Mr. Bartlett the owner. A fly only water located just off the A832 Muir of Ord /Ullapool road it is very convenient from the Beauly or Dingwall areas and is open 8am to 10 pm in the summer. **Sessions are £10, 4 hrs (4 fish), £7.50, 3 hrs (3 fish)** or £5, 2 hrs (2 fish) which must be great value dad! For Jean Bartlett does not charge for kids (wee kids). There is a discount for disabled and OAP'S. Picnic tables and seats give some little comfort while watching the Osprey treat the bag limit with much contempt. **Pre bookings, Tel: (01997) 433 219** See advertisement page 12

LOCH ACHILTY
Brown/Rainbow Trout, Boat/Fly only, Open all year, Dawn-dusk

A wonderfully located loch just off, but well hidden from the A835 west of Contin, opposite the Achilty Hotel. Splendid mature trees surrounding much of the shore line to provide numerous terrestrials to supplement the excellent hatches and profusion of snail and shrimp. Mark Butcher in his fourth year of consolidating this fine loch is knowledgable and enthusiast stocking only with best quality fish which produced a cracking 10lbr in 97'. There are eight boats for two rods each at **£10 per rod per 4 hrs (2 fish)** and pro rata for other periods with electric motors available at £1.25 an hour. Access is excellent with parking at the loch side. Rainbow to 10lb and Brownies to 5lb are the heavies with the addition of Orrin Blues and Arctic Char to 5lb in 1997/8, that however, is only part of the charm. This a quite beautiful place with songbirds, waterfowl and the occasional osprey to draw your interest and relax the mind. **Tel: (01997) 421245 or 521402.**
See advertisement page 12

RIVER CONON - BALLOAN HOUSE HOTEL WATER

This salmon and sea trout beat extends almost 1 mile from the old railway bridge at Achulty to the Rogie Falls with good trout fishing a bonus. Tel: David Jackson (01997) 433 440.

TARVIE LOCHS - TROUTMASTER FISHERY
Rainbow and Brown Trout - Open all year

This is a cracker, hence ***TROUTMASTER.*** Just 3 miles north of Contin on the Ullapool road (A862T) take a left at the sign, just one 1/2 mile on tarmac road reveals this secluded but easy access Highland loch of some splendour with mature foliage and trees to dress the heather covered hill surround. Parking is provided and there is lochside access for the disabled fisher. Loch an Eich Bhain is 25 acres and is boat fly fishing only. Loch Ruith a Phuill is smaller with bank fishing by fly or spinner, a most progressive management decision. The average for 1996 was 2lb 5 oz with fish less than 1 1/2lb being returned. A catch and release system operates when you have your limit. Rainbows to 15lb and brownies to 4lb have been introduced for 97'. However, it is the utter consistency of top quality fishing in wonderful Highland ambiance that has encouraged the exceptional number of returning anglers to these lochs. A dedicated fishers location there are no facilities for non fishers or children at the boat/fly loch. However, the bank fishing location is perfectly delightful for picnics, walking and bird watching, is quite rural with resident Roe and Red deer together with multitudinous bird life. Preferred fly fishing conditions are warm and bright days with a touch of breeze, though there are those who prefer close to glass surface and fish dry. There is no shortage of insect life, aquatic and terrestrial, with sedge creating the dry fly fishers dream for a shorter period than most would wish for. Traditional Highland flies are all you need here so long as you fish them in harmony with the existing conditions. **Invicta, G & H Sedge, Black Pennel, Soldier Palmer, and from early August on a light oatmeal Heather Moth** will do the trick. Advance reservations in the summer is advised since the maximum rods are 17 for boat and 15 for bank fishing. **Permits are available from:**

Morisons - West End, Beauly (01463) 782 213
Sports & Model Shop - Dingwall (01349) 862 346
Urray Post Office, Marybank (01997) 433 201
Graham's Inverness (01463) 233 178 & Nairn (01667) 455 009

Boat per rod: 4 hours (2 fish) £10.00	**8 hours (4 fish) £20.00**
Bank per rod: 4 hours (2 fish) £8.00	**8 hours (4 fish) £14.00**

Season discount cards at £5 allow £3 off boat and £2 off bank costs
Tarvie Lochs Fishery, Contin, Ross-shire IV14 9EJ (01997) 421250

ALNESS ANGLING CLUB
Full membership: £90.00
Senior citizens: £50.00
Juniors (under 16) : £20.00
Permits only from: J & M Patterson. High Street, Alness
Day permit: £12 - Junior (under 16) £6 - Father and junior £15
Weekly permit: (Mon-Sat) £40 - Junior £20 - Father/junior £50
Loch Morie £3.50 per day rod - Junior £2.50

No Sunday Fishing, No dogs or fire lighting permitted on any beat
There is some reorganisatin of fishing at time of going to press, so inquiries should be made locally for 1998.

With control of salmon and sea trout fishing on 3 beats totalling 3 miles of River plus the estuary of the River Averon and Loch Morie it is little wonder Alness is one of the most popular locations in Easter Ross. Some twenty miles long the Averon is a Highland spate river of easy access which enters the Cromarty firth close to Alness town Methods are restricted to unweighted fly or worm to be fished only with a fly rod and reel. An early run of Salmon is expected in March or April with the best fishing June through August when a grilse run starts and continues right into October with the bonus of a late 'Greyback' run. The nature of this river is that it takes hard drought to render the pools unfishable, the lower stretches holding early fish and all pools in residence from mid season Explicit regulations, access details and a good map are supplied with permit purchase.

RIVER AVERON (ALNESS)   **Season: 11 Feb - 15 October**
BEAT ONE: Fishing from the left bank only from the junction of the Blackwater to Inchlumpie pool where markers so indicate. Approach is from the road which passes through Ardross village off the A836. Fishing both fly or worm on a fly rod are permitted. This stretch holds a surprising number of sea trout.

BEAT TWO: Access to this double bank fishing is from the Struie Road. The upper limit is posted with the lower limit above the Bridge Pool in Alness. A footbridge crosses near the top. There is some good fly water here thanks to bank maintenance members.

BEAT THREE: *FLY ONLY* is the order of things on this beat which extends from the Alness Road bridge down to the swing bridge. Access is good with all pools fishable over a wide latitude of conditions.

ESTUARY BEAT: A separate permit is required for this beat which opens 1 April with *FLY ONLY* permitted until 1 May when worm on fly rod may be used.

LOCH MORIE: With salmon, sea trout, brown trout, ferox and char all vying for attention at some time in the season this loch offers very interesting fishing time for but a pittance.

NOVAR ESTATE WATERS

The estate has fishings on the River Averon (Alness), Glass and Lochs Glass and Morie in addition to three holiday cottages. The Averon salmon fishing is *FLY ONLY* and varies from £15 to £45 per day rod. Trout fishing on lochs allows fly, worm or spinning from the bank or from boats available only on Loch Morie. For further details Tel: (01349) 830 208.

STONEYFIELD LOCHS TROUT FISHERY
A "TROUTMASTER WATER"
Rainbow/ Brown Trout - Open all year - 9am till 10pm/dusk

A new fishery opened in 1996 by owners John and Jennifer Connell has two lochs and is situated just off the A9 north of Alness. Take a right at the Newmore/Invergordon junction and the fishery is to your left at the sign at the top of the hill. A 5 acre loch is fly only while bait fishing is permitted on the smaller 3 acre water. Stocked with both brown and rainbow trout of 2lb or better there are also double figure fish to challenge your skill with catch and release permitted after limits are reached. There is a hut and toilet on site with disabled access where snacks, rod rental and flies available.

2 Hrs one fish £6.00 4 Hrs two fish £10.00 8 Hrs four fish £16.00
Sport C&R ticket £8.00 for 8 hrs.
Prebooking Tel: (01349) 852 632 See advertisement page 13

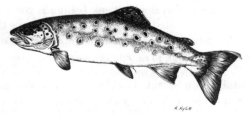

R.Kyle

9

LOCH EYE

Only a few minutes drive from the Royal Town of Tain this lovely loch which is one mile long by half a mile across lies in the rolling coastal plains of Easter Ross in secluded surroundings of a bird sanctuary where geese, coot, swans, and duck are in residence, while inquisitive otters and stealth osprey treat the bag limit with some degree of contempt. The loch is stream and spring fed and retains excellent levels even in high summer drought. A shallow loch, evenings in summer can be the best time for rises as the air cools and shadows lengthen. Only boat fishing (without motors) is permitted and a 10 fish limit prevails on each boat although there is no limit on the number of trout which may be returned. The average is close to the 1lb mark with several of 2lb taken each season, in fact, ideal table fish. Traditional Scottish hill loch flies are the normal attractors although some nice catches have been taken with mini-muddlers and buzzers. This is all very exclusive and definitely not just run of the mill. There are three boats available which for the princely sum of £15.00 allow one or two rods to fish from dawn till dusk. **For Loch Eye and Kyle of Sutherland Permits, Fishing tackle, Quality Guns and experienced advice: R. Macleod & Son - Fishing Tackle. Tain. Tel: (01862) 892171**

FISH
THE
TARVIE LOCHS

ROSS-SHIRE's FIRST TROUTMASTER WATER

STOCKED RAINBOWS TO 15LB; BROWNS TO 6LB

MAIN LOCH BOAT AND FLY FISHING ONLY, SEPARATE
LOCH AVAILABLE FOR BANK FISHING USING FLY OR
COARSE METHODS

OPEN ALL YEAR 9 A.M. TO DUSK OR 10 P.M.

TACKLE HIRE & FLIES FOR SALE

R.E.F.F.I.S. & S.T.A.N.I.C. APPROVED INSTRUCTOR
(BY APPOINTMENT ONLY)

Member of the Association of Scottish Stillwater Fisheries

FOR BOOKING & DETAILS CONTACT:
THE TARVIE LOCHS TROUT FISHERY
TARVIE, CONTIN, BY STRATHPEFFER, ROSS-SHIRE IV14 9EJ
TEL: 01997 421250
INTERNET:
http://www.erack.Com/tands/Fishing Places/Scotland/Tarvie.htm.

13

other *FISHING SCOTLAND* guides

Inverness-shire - Isle of Skye - Moray & Nairn

Argyll, the Isles, Loch Lomond, Stirling & Trossachs

HIGHLAND ANGLING SERVICES

Highland Angling Services should be your first stop if you want to learn fly fishing for trout. One day and short breaks with B & B or hotel accommodation as required are totally inclusive of transport from accommodation, all tackle, fishing permits and boat with motor where required. Bob and Sue Brighton have been established since 1992 so have considerable experience and local knowledge to get you hooked on fly fishing. Give them a call.   See below.

PART TWO
WESTER ROSS
RIVER CARRON & LOCH DUGHAILL - ACHNASHELLACH

It would appear that the new owner is not making any fishing available – for 1998 at least.

LOCH DAMPH - LOCH TORRIDON HOTEL

The A896 crosses the River Balgy which empties into Loch Torridon from this just out of sight loch some two miles from this fine hotel. Recent returns are unconfirmed and it appears that only bank fishing permits are available from the hotel. Tel: (01445) 791 242.

LOCH LOINE and LOCH COULTRIE

Both of these lochs contain multitudes of typical hill loch trout with the occasional salmon in Coultrie. A short walk (5 minutes max) from the A896. Permits may be available from Pattinson, Tel: (015200 733 227

RIVER BALGY - TIGH AN EILEAN HOTEL - SHIELDAIG

A short steep river with fishing for 2 rods at £22.50 each occasionally available Tuesday, Thursday and Saturday. Tel: (01520) 755251.

15

KINLOCHEWE ANGLING ASSOCIATION

This village club has a very nice selection of brown trout lochs set in some of the finest wild Highland scenery anywhere and charges the pittance of £2 per rod day to fish them. Permits and local knowledge are available from the Glen Docharty Craft Shop in the village.

Loch Bharanaichd

Just off the A 896 Torridon road about 4 miles from the village there is a short walk over peat bog to the loch. There are no restrictions and the wee troot are free risers to any of the traditional flies of a black or dark colour. Any time from late April these fish are in great condition and fight like the deil'. Size wise you can count on maybe 3 to the pound with an odd 1/2 lbr for your own breakfast, grand stuff these trout.

Loch a' Chroisg

Another almost roadside loch this time on the A832 towards Achnasheen. There is a nice shingle shore here and the wee craters of around the 1/2lb tend to forage in the shallows so be sneaky and play the cool approach. This is a good place for a picnic with plenty of safe space for kids.

Kinlochewe Hill Lochs

Just the thing to work up an appetite for fried trout. These lochs are a short strenuous walk to 900 ft just behind the village. There is every likelihood you will see no one all day be amazed by the quiet and justly surprised by the bird life. A pair of eagles or a group of red deer might be your only observer. The wee troot will be of 2 or 3 to the pound and give you a run for your £2 permit out performing your 1lb put and take rainbow.

SHEILDAIG LODGE HOTEL FISHERIES

3 miles south of Gairloch village, Shieldaig Lodge controls fishing of a number of roadside and hill trout lochs Tel: (01445) 741 250

LOCH MAREE & TRIBUTARIES

In the most spectacular of Highland mountain, loch and river ambiance the A832 Kinlochewe to Gairloch road follows the south west shore line for almost 2/3rd the length of the 14 mile long Loch Maree, so famous in the tales and reminiscences of large sea trout. Though well fed by run off from the steep slopes along each shore line Loch Maree's main tributaries are the River Kinlochewe which runs in at the south east end it's self fed by Lochs Coulin, Clair the Glendocharty Burn and Heights River.

LOCH MAREE

Salmon & Sea Trout   **Season: 11 Feb - 12 Oct**

'Classic' is perhaps the best way to describe this long narrow loch and the **Loch Maree Hotel** so Highland in vision and surroundings. Fishing is organised into beats some of which are rotated allowing the experience of fishing extensive stretches of water. Best favoured areas for salmon are around the islands and the head of the loch at Kinlochewe early on. From boat bay on the south shore over to Fhasaigh Burn and all the way to the head of the loch is superb water from shore to shore so set drifts are of little consequence. Salmon are regularly taken here even after sea trout appear from July on. Best sea trout drifts at the head of the loch are the north and south shores, off the river mouth and where wee burns join the loch. The other end of the loch has to be fished in traditional style close to the shore where the shallows shelf into deep water. The top beats for sea trout have by tradition been around the islands and are much sought after by experiences anglers from all corners of the world. The magnificent passed runs of sea trout have diminished, big heavies of up to almost 20lb are being searched for still, such are memories. However, some increased catches of sea trout in 96/97 up to 8lb is welcome news that brightens the horizon of expectation. The season is under way and running by mid April with salmon the quarry until early July when sea trout are expected to be making their presence felt. Wet flies fished in train with a **big bushy Black Pennel** on the bob are quite likely to bring on the action with **Invicta and Soldier Palmer** a productive supporting cast. Dapping the fly however, does most of the attracting on this loch. Again the **Black Pennel** is a mighty well favoured dressing vying very close with the **Daddy Long legs** (Cranefly) in popularity. The certainty of rising sea trout with the dapped fly makes the preparation worth while for there can be no greater fishing pleasure than the intensity and expectation after the first silver fish has crashed at your fly, and gone! Bank fishing is not permitted and boats are at a premium as the season proceeds from June through August when pre reservations are a wise choice. Neil MacDonald, Bridge House, Kinlochewe Tel: (01445) 760 264 has a boat at £25 a day for two rods. **Loch Maree Hotel** with pier adjacent has a fleet of boats with engines and experienced ghillies. For details of accommodation and fishing contact: **The Manager, Loch Maree Hotel, Wester Ross. IV22 2HN**
Tel: (01445) 760 288   **See advertisement page 18**

Loch Maree Hotel

ACHNASHEEN WESTER ROSS IV22 2HN
Tel: 01445 760 288

Catering for anglers and tourists since it was built in 1872, the Hotel is situated between Gairloch and Kinlochewe on the southern shore of Loch Maree. There is no place cradled in lovelier surroundings. All bedrooms now have private bath or shower, all are now centrally heated and fully equipped with television, direct dial telephone and tea and coffee making facilities.

With such unspoilt scenery, the scope for hill walking or mountaineering is tremendous. Of course you don't have to be an expert survivalist to enjoy the wildest countryside in Britain. Even the gentlest of walks can be the most rewarding with the breathtaking views, and wildlife and plants you may see.

Gairloch, some 9 miles north west of the Hotel sports a 9 hole Golf Course, with glorious views over the sea to Skye.

The isolated and unspoiled countryside, once home to Wolves and Bears, still remains a haven for Deer, Pinemartens, Otters, Wild Cats and many other rare species. Ornithologists will find the Golden Eagle, Buzzards, Ospreys, Ptarmigan, Capercaillie, Black Throated Divers and Crossbills along with many other summer visiting migrants to the area.

Loch Maree is legendary among fishermen, principally because the Loch has produced the largest sea trout in Great Britain and also because it is set in the most outstanding scenery in the Western Highlands. The season is from April until October, the busy period being July and August when early bookings are recommended. Boat fishing, two rods to a boat with a ghillie provided, is from the pier below the Hotel. Dapping, wet and dry fly are the methods of fishing practised here. Spinning is permitted until 1st July.

The Hotel has eight available boats all with a ghillie (mandatory). We are also able to arrange fishing for Salmon and Brown Trout locally, when weather conditions and availability permit. The Hotel has a well-equipped boathouse for rod storage, a small tackle shop and excellent drying and boot room facilities.

GAIRLOCH - POOLEWE - ALTBEA

A browse over any map of Wester Ross might well relay the vast expanse of mountain and glen decked with garlands of lochs from puddle to massive. The Gairloch **Tourist Information Centre (01445) 712 130** has staff well able to provide information and answers on all matters of this community with Golf, pony-trekking, sea fishing, sailing and canoeing available locally. West Highland Marine on Pier Road supply all manner of boats, canoes, sea and freshwater fishing tackle. Poolewe at the head of Loch Ewe which the River Ewe enters in its short run from Loch Maree is unique with semitropical plants and palm trees, a remarkable fact in view of Poolewe's position close to the 58th parallel, which cut through Siberia and Hudsons Bay! The majestic scenery takes some beating without even leaving the well surfaced roads. Aultbea "the burn of the birches" is a community strung out along a sheltered bay where the **Aultbea Hotel** overlooks the Isle of Ewe and is just a couple of miles on the A832 from Laide village on the shores of Gruinard Bay with its wonderful unspoiled silver beachs. There are hotels, self catering cottages, **Gruinard Bay Caravan Park** where fishing permits are issued, a Post Office (with fishing tackle), village shops, a pub, in fact all anyone needs to enjoy life.

THE GAIRLOCH ANGLING CLUB WATERS

Various lochs and a small river which are available to the visitor by day permit under the terms of certain regulations may well change during the season so ask locally what the current situation is regarding access. In this wild area it is easy to dismiss as of no consequence ones presence on the hill. Shooting, lambing and other hill work are important to the success of the seasons work and on occasions require that others leave certain areas prepared for that work. Responsible fishers, hillwalkers, or just walk about people have interest in and respect for those who work in such wild places and always ask permission before going on the hill. **Permits** are available from The Chandlers, Pier Road; The Post Office, Pier Road; K. Gunn, Newsagent and Tackle; Taylors General Store, Poolewe. Ghillie services, casting instruction and rental equipment is available from D. W. Roxborough, Gairloch, IV21 2BP Tel: (01445) 712 057

LOCHS TOLLAIDH (Tollie) & BOOR
Boat £8 per day + £2 per rod (max 2) - Bank fishing £2 per day
Tollie is accessible direct from the A832 about half way between Gairloch and Poolewe. Just full of wild trout they are of the usual two to the pound with a few each day close to the 1lb mark. They are free risers and come on early with May through July being most productive. Spinning and bank fishing is permitted with the side opposite the road well favoured. **Boor Loch** on the opposite side of the road from Tollie has a plentiful population of wee troot and is of easy safe access. All dark traditional flies are good attractors here.

LOCH GARBHAIG - Boat or bank fishing
Access to this loch is via a forestry road signposted Victoria Falls and Power Station off the A832 towards Kinlochewe. From the car park it is a good 30 minute uphill walk via a locked gate. The trout are wild and of around the 1lb if you can move them. The reputation is that the crystal clear water allows them sight of all but the stealth fisher. A beautiful isolated location where quiet prevails.

LOCHS BAD NA SCALAIG - DUBH & AM FEUR
Boat £8 per day + £4 per rod (max 2) - Bank fishing £4 per day
This typical chain of connected hill lochs is accessible and convenient being just by the roadside of the A832 south of Gairloch. This is a good loch system to take non fishers or for a family picnic with good parking and beautiful scenery. Stocked on occasions by the club there are some big boy's in here much better than your average loch. The loch is subject to fluctuation due to hydro operations and like all enlarged waters fishes best when the level is low. From May on this is FLY ONLY from bank or boat with spinning permitted until then. There are pike in these lochs which doubtless help to reduce the usual surplus of very wee troot. The channel to Dubh Loch, the dam and waterfall are all good areas with the tiny Am Feur Loch reputed to hold oversized trout and pike.

LOCH SQUOD
There is no availability of fishing to the Gairloch Angling Club for 1998.

GAIRLOCH HILL LOCHS - Bank fishing only - £2 per rod day

An Ordinance survey map, a compass and the ability to read and navigate is recommended here as for most Highland hill loch excursions. By the very nature of such fishings one should expect that the free taking trout will be of 2 or 3 to the pound with no surprise if a 1lb or indeed 5lb brownie should decide to give you combat. Many of this type of loch have weed problems these days, such is the case with **Lochs Clair** and **an t-Sabhail-mhoineas**, however, that's what it is all about and such conditions certainly extend ones ability if not vocabulary. Do not be shy to cast a dry fly if there is not much free water and try one anyway if the surface is close to unmoved by breeze especially in the evening. The country about you here is spectacular with nuance in scent and colour unmatched anywhere - to additionally fish here may be the closest you will come to heaven. There follows here a list of the club hill lochs with their grid reference.

Loch Airigh Mhic Criadh 830765 Loch Clair 820756
Loch an t-Sabhail-mhoine 820763 Loch Airigh a'Phuill 842756
Loch nam Buainichean 853735 Loch Dhu na beiste 863732
Loch na Feithe Mugaig 860747 Loch Doire na h-Airghe 870740

RIVER KERRY - Salmon - Fly only - Season: 11 Feb - 15 Oct

For a reasonable £12 per rod day with a maximum of 4 rods one can enjoy the pleasures of fishing a most attractive river with unique features found only in the west Highlands. Though the river exits from Loch Bad fish are now prevented access due to power station systems. A run of fish with June spates would be the expected start of the migration with mid July through August expected to be most productive. Salmon have in the past out numbered sea trout even when these silver fish arrived almost in excess. Salmon still provide great sport in 17 named pools and numerous other productive stretches. Fish of 10 to 12lb are common with the average in the 41/2 to 61/2 lb class. There is quite a bit of natural undergrowth to avoid when casting so an 11ft rod would be perfect for most fishers. Size 8 and 10 flies are right in any Scottish dressings though the writer would be more specific and fish Blue Charm or Hairy Mary tubes. Permits for the river are issued daily at the Craig Mor Hotel, Gairloch. (01445) 712068

LETTEREWE ESTATE FISHINGS
Fionn loch - Brown trout - fly only

This, one of the very best wild brown trout lochs in the Highlands is remotely situated on the Letterewe Estate which strictly controls vehicle access to the loch. A track suitable only for 4-wheel drive vehicles runs from Poolewe and is monitored from the keepers cottage at Kernsary. The Gairloch club has previously had a boat and a 4-wheel drive available to visitors, however there will be no such facilities for visitors in 1996. An alternative is to deal direct with Letterewe Estate. Those who have fished this loch are all of one mind, that the superb wilderness mountain location and the fishing are exceptional. Fish are of around the 1/2lb on average, however, on a good day you maybe return 10 brownies keeping a few up to 1lb. The largest of the brownies here are huge and of course it is these wild creatures that we all dream of. Its a rocky loch where care must be taken with an experienced ghillie recommended. Boat-house bay, Sandy bay on the opposite side and the head of the north end are productive drifts as is the majority of the shore line. Dapping is favoured, especially for the big fish though wet flies of Ke-he, Black Zulu, Invicta and a Black Pennel on the bob bring on plenty of action. The estate has some most attractive quality self-catering accommodations for rent which include: Little Gruinard House, with salmon fishing on the Little Gruinard; Heights of Kinlochewe with a boat on Loch Maree; Ardlair House with hill loch fishing including Loch Fionn. For details contact: Mrs Barbara Grant, the Head Stalker's wife, Letterewe, Loch Maree, Wester Ross IV22 2HH. (01445) 760 207

RIVER EWE - Salmon & Sea Trout - Season: 11 Feb - 30 Sept

The River Ewe flows from the north west end of Loch Maree as the link to the sea through which all of those magnificent sea trout and salmon have travelled. The River Ewe takes a mite over a mile to work its way first through some slow narrows which need freshet conditions to fish well, then through a series of short tumbling rapids with Tee Pool, Macordies, which have produced salmon in excess of 20lb in recent seasons and Hen, Manse, and Flats all excellent holding pools. The stream splits round an island to merge again just before entering the much favoured tidal Sea Pool. Salmon run early and it is usual to take fish on opening day with sporadic increase of arriving fish taking till late June to be considered resident in numbers. Sea trout are not expected in strength until early June. Garry Dog, Silver Stoats Tail, Hairy Mary, Blue Charm and Dark Mackerel all do well. Though occasional day permits become available this is a river that requires advance booking. Further details from The Keeper, Keepers Cottage, River Ewe, Poolewe, Wester Ross.

AULTBEA ESTATES HILL LOCH FISHING

The estate trout lochs are far too numerous to mention individually in detail, however the permit contains map information with some of the larger lochs plotted on the permit with access details. Sheet 19 OS is recommended if you want to access any of the more remote loch where the best fishing is to be had. The broon troot of course vary from loch to loch to some degree with many being chock fu' o' wee craters of three to the pound and make the day for someone just learning to fly cast for these fish are not shy and will take on anything even vaguely resembling a fly. Bank fishing permits are £2.50 a day; £12 a week; £25 for the season. Permits are issued by: Laide Post Office (01445) 731 252; **Gruinard Bay Caravan Park Tel: (01445) 731 225**; Bridgend Stores (01445) 720 227; Highland Lodges Aultbea (01445) 731 268; and Old Smiddy Holidays (01445) 731 425 who have boats on some lochs at £10 a day. The following is just a wee taster of what is out there.

LOCH na BEISTE

Sitting close to the Laide/Mellon Udrigle road at the junction with the small road that branches for Loch Slaggan this is just a fine loch if you have non fishers in tow or have to encourage someone new to fly casting for there are no shortage of takers here, sometimes two at a time and it takes maybe three of the wild creatures to make up a pound. Fishes well from late April though late May and June would be preferred. There is usualy a boat here though bank fishing is quite fine.

LOCH SLAGGAN

Take the wee road which leaves the Laide/ Mellon Udrigle road by na Beiste and you will find the loch to the left. Again there is no shortage of brownies in this one of the larger lochs on the Peninsula and the average is maybe two and a bit to the pound with an odd 3/4 lbr really making waves. From early May these trout are in fine fettle and will give you a surprise with their crash takes and determined dives. There is always at least one boat here with no specific drifts since most of the water is productive particularly the east side near the wee island.

LOCH a' BHAIDLUACHRAICH (GOOSE LOCH)

To the south west of Aultbea and accessed by way of the road past Drumchork Lodge then by path alongside the Allte Beiste for about a mile to this the largest loch in the area. The numerous inhabitants again provide excellent sport with good baskets sufficient for a whole family breakfast. Frequent fish over the 1lb mark come from bank fishing the many bays and burn mouths when there has been a freshet, An easy shore to traverse and wonderful for a whole day walk about.

LOCH an ERSKE

With a walk of about half a mile from the Mellon Charles road this loch has reputation of large trout which of course are very difficult to catch. It is said that those who fish this regularly may not come up with a high number of fish but that the average is certainly over the 1lb mark. So, any time from early May go improve your weight return average. Enjoy.

LOCH BEN DHEARG

An easy walk from Loch an Erske with more large fish that come into condition by late April and provide best fishing when a good wave breaks the surface. These last two lochs are certainly for the experienced fly fisher with the patience and fortitude.

ULLAPOOL

This vibrant fishing village which lies on a narrow peninsula extending into Loch broom was founded by the Fisheries Association in 1788 to further the herring industry. There is safe anchorage for all manner of craft with rental of everything from row boats to day cruisers available. Situated among some of the finest scenery of the western Highlands Ullapool is an ideal centre from which to tour and explore the many glens, Mountains and coastal scenery. The region is well served with an excellent road system which allows for easy travel and enjoyable experiences of the magnificent grandeur of Wester Ross. The **Tourist Information Centre** in **Argyll Street**, just beside the Police Station, is ready and able to help with all your inquiries of accommodation or what to see first! There are innumerous self-catering and full service accommodations and cottages in this area with the **Harbour Lights Hotel** which overlooks the harbour and Loch Broom catering for anglers. The Ullapool Angling Club has access to various loch fishing and make daily permits available to visitors from: Lochbroom Hardware, Shore Street who also carry some fishing tackle and **Mountain Man Supplies** on **Argyll Street** who are fully equipped tackle merchants and sports outfitters.

ULLAPOOL ANGLING CLUB - Fly only
Permits: £4.00 per day - £20 per week - Senior citizens 1/2 price
Juniors (under 16) 1/2 price

The Strath Kanaird Hill Lochs situated to the north of Ullapool are a group of 3 lochs managed by the club. Approached by a gated road which is steep and winding and partly tarmac surfaced it is Not suitable for caravans or large campers. **Loch Beinn Dearg** holds natural brown trout and was stocked from 1992 through 1995 with rainbow trout. **Loch na Maoile** again with natural brown trout was for some reason stocked with salmon and char of 2 to 3lb in 1993. Apparently the salmon lasted two winters and occasional char are still taken. Juniors (under 16) are permitted to spin this loch. **Loch Dubh** which has not been stocked has retained its natural brownies which are reputed to be much better and heavier that in the other lochs! There are boats on these lochs, however, they are for the use of locals only? You are likely to find the trout of around 2 or 3 to the pound with an odd surprise of maybe a pound. Usual Highland hill loch flies are fine with Black Spider, Black Pennel, Peter

Ross and Zulu being the local choice. Do not forget to take a wee bushy light oatmeal Heather moth with you from late July on when they clear everything else off the menu.

MOUNTAIN MAN SUPPLIES

Located in the old Ullasport building **Mountain Man Supplies** is a breath of fresh air in outdoor activity supplies to Ullapool. Completely renovated and ready for the 1998 season it is jammed to the gunnels with all that is best in mountaineering, hillwalking, backpacking, camping and survival equipment not to mention an extensive fishing department with everything from kids rod sets to top of the range graphite rods and all those in between. Permits for local Association waters are available and also for private beats. Trout fishing on **Loch Achall** at the head of the River Ullapool just 2 1/2 miles from the town has bank (£6.00 per day) or boat fishing (£15.00 per day) and is **FLY ONLY**. The location is very Highland and your only likely company will be sika or red deer. The Upper Kanaird River beat is some seven miles north of the town from where the A835 crosses the river and upstream to the bridge just below Langwell Lodge. Eleven good pools make this good value at £15.00 to £20.00 per rod per day with a £5.00 deposit returned when you hand in your catch return - Fish or no fish.
Tel: (01854) 613 383   **See advertisement on page 26**

INVERPOLLY ESTATE FISHINGS

Even the most travelled Highland mountaineer, angler, hill walker and explorer of Scottish wilderness praise the grandeur of this area with Stac Polly and a hundred loch and lochan fed splashing crystal burns and streams, all with most splendid coastal perimeters where blue ocean meets the golden western sky each evening at setting sun. What an easy job the photographer has with PR photography here in Northern Wester Ross. Various fishings together with either a self-catering lodge or a cottage are available May through September. The main fishing is on the Rivers Polly and Osaig with boats on Lochs Soinascaig and Badagyle and Lurgainn are available by casual day permit at £14 per day or bank fishing for £5. Brochure and information: Polly Estates Ltd Inverpolly, Ullapool, Ross-shire IV26 2YB. Tel: (01854) 622452.

PART THREE
SUTHERLAND

Although it seems remote, it's very easy to reach the most westerly and northern corners of this vast expanse of Highland mountain, river, and glen where to eastward the moors of the flow country gradually soften towards Caithness with its precipitous coastal splendour. The roads may be narrower than in the south, however they are of excellent condition and follow long proven paths and cattle trails which merge at important towns and villages some of which have long since passed into history. Some people visit the wide open spaces to push themselves to the limit, others come to relax with the diverse range of enticing, invigorating and enjoyable things to do. Walking in the spectacular mountain areas of the west or the rolling moors of the east attracts visitors from all corners of the globe. Visiting ancient places where the heritage of the nation was moulded allows one to wonder at the communications and travel of old when this place truly was remote. The historian will find more to answer than one holiday can contain, **Inchnadamph** is just one mecca for the geologist with underground caves and evidence of man from the last ice age, **Lochinver** a prosperous 17th and 18th century fishing village with an expanded harbour industry based on a £6.5 million white fish and shellfish program with the Assynt Crofters 3 years into an enterprising cooperative these are just two of the diverse life styles that flourish today in this wild country.

KYLE OF SUTHERLAND

In the heartland of Scotland's Northern Highlands the Kyle of Sutherland is the ideal base for salmon, sea trout and brown trout fishing. The Kyle consists of 600 square miles of beauty, history, rivers, forests, and glens stretching from east of Ederton almost to Ledmore in the west and to the north of Loch Shin. Club and association waters are available by day permit throughout the region additional to some of the finest and expensive river beats. There are two principal tackle stores who also issue various fishing permits, **Macleod & Son in Tain (01862) 892171** and **Sutherland Sporting Company in Lairg (01549) 402 229**. There are hotels, guest houses, B & B, caravan and camping parks to suit all pockets some of which have there own fishing or can arrange this with due notice. **Dornoch** and **Lairg** have **Tourist Information Centres** where you will be pointed in the right direction of all your inquiries. The

Mallin House Hotel on Church Street Dornoch (01862) 810 335 is always keen to look after fisher folk. **Dornoch Lochans (01862) 810 600** is a stocked rainbow fishery and a putting course on the outskirts of the town in very beautiful surroundings. The **Dunroamin Hotel** on **Lairg Road, Bonar Bridge (01863) 766 236** have a very popular public bar additional to full hotel services and a disabled access self catering flat. On the A837 Lairg to Lochinver Road at the head of Strath Oykel the **Oykel Bridge Hotel** has famous trout fishing and self catering cottages while just 11/2 miles from Ledmore is **Altnacealgach Inn (01854) 666 260** next to **Altnacealgach Motel (01854) 666 220** on the shores of **Loch Borralan** with first class brown trout and char fishing. 20 miles north of Lairg on the A836 at the west end of the famous Loch Naver is the **Altnaharra Hotel** equally famous as a fishing hostelry with a dinning room of note.

KYLE OF SUTHERLAND ANGLING ASSOCIATION

Kyle Salmon & Sea Trout season: **1 June - 30 September**
Loch Brown Trout fishing season: **15 march - 6 October**

Fishing on the Kyle is available using any legal tackle - Fly, spinner or bait except for the 3 small areas which are designated **FLY ONLY**. Low cost day permits for sea trout fishing in the estuary below Bonar Bridge - do **NOT** cover Upper Kyle fishing. Kyle fishing starts from the bridge upwards, on both banks. The first **FLY ONLY** area begins on the south bank immediately above Bonar Bridge and extends to Invercharron Point. A mile upstream from Bonar Bridge the Kyle widens to form the "Meikle Pool", before narrowing again at the village of Culrain below Carbisdale Castle. Just over a mile upstream is the second **FLY ONLY** section at the junction of the River Shin. The third **FLY ONLY** point is just over 7 miles further upstream where the renowned Oykel and the Cassley Rivers join the Kyle at the end of association water. Best fished on a receding tide the Kyle provides what can only be described as excellent and varied fishing on fine fast flowing runs of ideal fly water. Wading is generally comfortable although a wading staff is recommended since the current can be very strong. July through September are best with catches of two or more salmon and numerous sea and brown trout per rod per tide a common result. Even when drought conditions effect the neighbouring rivers the Kyle still fishes well. Favoured flies are Munro Killer, Willie Gunn and Hairy Mary.

LOCH MIGDALE - Brown Trout - Bait and spinning permitted

Set among the rolling hills and woodlands above Bonar Bridge this most attractive loch is very easy accessible and the ideal location for a family picnic or outing. Proceed straight up the steep hill in front of you as you cross to the north side of the Bonar bridge. The loch will appear on your right at about 1/2 mile, continue to the sign 'Loch Migdale' by the church. This is a great loch with free rising trout whither you bank or boat fish it.

LOCH LAGGAN - OS sheet 21 Grid ref 660955

Easily accessible by car this typical Highland loch is inhabited by the expected 2 or 3 to the pound native trout. Continue past the 'Loch Migdale' sign for about 3 miles, Laggan is the next loch on the right, turn through the gate opposite the letter box and follow the track to the loch. Very suitable for family picnics in beautiful surroundings. The gravelly bay at the far side is good but stealth anywhere works best and fish are taken all over the loch. Some salmon enter the loch late on so be prepared.

Dornoch A A also issue permits and have a boat here.

LOCH LARGO - OS sheet 21 Grid ref 610995

Pass the 'Loch Laggan' turn off by 750 meters, turn left at a wooden gate. Follow the rough track to a fork at about a mile and park. Walk the left fork for a mile and a half to the loch. The wee fat trout are of about 1/2lb on average and as pleasant to sport with as the walk out of about 40 minutes.. Peace perfect peace and maybe an odd hill bird to sing while you lunch. **Dornoch A A also issue permits and have a boat here.**

LOCH CRACAIL MHOR - OS sheet 16 ref 625020

Magnificent Highland scenery and strong wild loch trout will make this excursion one you will remember. By pass the 'Largo' fork and carry straight on. Park at the inhabited croft at about one mile. Follow the track beyond the gate for another mile bypassing Loch Cracail Beig (on the right) which is not association water. Cracail Mhor is a very shallow loch with a reputation for beautifully marked trout with a high average of close to 3/4lb with indication of some really heavy browns. With such shallow clear water it is again stealth which makes the difference between a breakfast of trout and the thought that maybe there are no fish in't. Care is required since there are skerries about 1/3 of the way up the loch and off the north shore. **Dornoch A A also have a boat here. Bank fishing is prohibited**

LOCH BUIDH

Follow the Loch Migdale road for 5 miles to the loch on the left by the roadside. Some 30 ft deep in places there are both salmon and sea trout runs into the loch in the autumn. A pleasant place to fish with nice bank walking and always a fine breeze.

All of these lochs provide good sport to traditional Scottish flies of size 10 through 14 dependant on the wave running. Sure fire attractors are Black Pennel, Grouse and Claret, Soldier Palmer and Heather Fly in June followed by the Moth from late July. If the loch water just happens to be undisturbed by breeze try stalking your trout with a wee dry Badger just twitching on the surface, works magic.

Kyle fishing: £18 per rod day or £90 per rod weekly
Sea Trout: £3 per rod day or £15 per rod season
Loch boat Fishing - 2 rods: day £15 - week £40- extra rod £3
Bank fishing: £3 per day or £12 per week
Permits available from: R. Macleod & Son - Fishing Tackle Tain
Ardgay Shopping - Ardgay
Tourist Information Centres - Dornoch & Lairg
Strath Enterprises - Bonar Bridge (The only boat permit outlet)

LOCH SHIN - Brown Trout - Season: 15 April - 30 September
Loch Shin, the largest freshwater loch in Sutherland is 16 miles long and of very easy access the A838 Lairg to Laxford Bridge road never far from the shore. There is a dam just north of the village, with a small attractive loch below and a fish pass to permit migratory fish access. Lairg village has hotels, B & B, guest houses, a caravan park, and shops including **The Sutherland Sporting Company,** which carries a full stock of fishing tackle, country clothing and issues permits for Loch Shin and Lairg hill loch trout fishing with occasional rods available for river salmon fishing. Loch Shin Cruises & Fishing just north of Lairg on the A838 at Shinness hire fishing and cruising boats by the hour, day or week. **The Falls of Shin Visitor Centre** at the salmon leap is a not to be missed attraction that will keep you coming back. The **Lairg Angling Club** was formed in 1960, has 9 boats available from the club warden who can be found from the crack of dawn at the club hut at the

Lairg end of the loch and is the man to listen to regarding 'whats taking'. Brown trout are of about 8 oz. on average with perhaps 2 or 3 a day up to the 1lb mark and of course as on all big lochs the occasional huge fish. Bank fishing and spinning is permitted throughout the loch with no real need for known drifts, due to the depth of the loch it fishes best close to the shore. Favoured flies are Black Pennel, Silver Invicta, Black Zulu, and Kate MacLaren in size 10 & 12 with 8s if there are white tops to the waves. A fairly late loch the best time is from the last 2 weeks of June through July. When a warm westerly breaks the surface the loch fishes best till around mid day and then again from late afternoon into dusk. **Bank permits:** £5 per day or £15 per week. **Boats:** £10.00 per day (no rod charge) Outboards: £12 per day. **Permits** available from: **Dunroamin Caravan & Camping Park; The Sutherland Sporting Company, Lairg.** **See advertisement page 34**

LAIRG HILL LOCHS - FLY ONLY
LOCHS CRAGGIE & BEANNACH - Boat x 2 rods £15.00
LOCHS DOLA - TIGH NA GRIEGE - Boat x 2 rods £10.00

Returns indicated here should be considered in the light of the '95 drought.

Loch Craggie   1993 = 621; 94 = 507; 95 = 405
Loch Dola   1993 = 476; 94 = 455; 95 = 300

Perhaps the best known of local hill lochs, Craggie is reckoned to produce wild brown trout of the 2lb class with some consistency, this perhaps due to odd outcrops of limestone in this region. Boat fishing is the method with a liberal bag limit of 10 fish to 2 rods - No bank fishing. The season is 1 May to 30 September, however, it is generally late May before any real warmth of air and water bring on other than very selective activity. The locations and altitude are such that it is rare to experience a complete lack of wind, warm north westerlies being favoured. A 3/4lb average is not unreasonable to expect with a good day producing a couple over the 1lb mark. The hills above Lairg are a joy to behold with easy access, a great location to be accompanied by non fishers or for a family picnic. Permits and access details from: **The Sutherland Sporting Company, Lairg. Tel: (01549) 402 229; Dunroamin Caravan & Camping Park. Tel: (01549) 402 447 also have permits for Loch Craggie.**

INVERSHIN HOTEL

Overlooking the Kyles of Sutherland on the A836 halfway between Lairg and Bonar Bridge there is a 1/2 mile of great trout fishing on the very doorstep that goes free to resident guests. The proprietors, Brett and Alex Richards encourage anglers with the offer of early breakfast, packed lunches and late dinners. They can also arrange fishing for salmon and sea trout or brown trout on lochs in the area or on the Kyles of Sutherland. Tel: (01549) 421 202. **See advertisement on page 40**

FALLS OF SHIN VISITOR CENTRE
RIVER SHIN SALMON LEAP

Fisher or not there is little doubt the Shin Falls are perhaps the best place in the country to see salmon leap the rapids on their way upstream. The scenic beauty of the glen is wonderful so do not forget your camera.
The visitor centre perched above the falls in a mature treed backdrop is tops with locals and visitors such is the attraction of the forest walks, the kids activity playground, the popular restaurant, a shop overflowing with all sorts of gifts. **See the advertisement page 39**

RIVER SHIN

A stretch of river adjacent to the Visitor Centre is let by the day from 1 July through August and September. There are normally three rods available at £27.50 each or £65 for all three per day. Details from Willie Pirritt Tel: (01549) 441 236 or Sutherland Sporting Company, Lairg.

OYKEL BRIDGE HOTEL & SELF CATERING COTTAGES
WILD BROWN TROUT FISHING

This renowned angling hotel has fishing on many excellent trout lochs set in wonderful Highland grandeur around Strath Oykel and Ledmore. There is, additional to full service hotel accommodation three comfortable self catering cottages each in secluded situations with private road access and sleeping up to six. The wild trout are prolific in these waters, average two to the pound with maybe two in every basket of 12 to 15 trout being over the one pound mark. There are also Ferox and char in some of these waters which are taken mainly by trolling, though fly fishing is the preferred method of fishing these lochs. For more information and Brochure **See advertisement on page 41**

ALTNAHARRA HOTEL FISHING
Salmon, sea trout, wild brown trout, ferox & char
Season: 1 March - 15 October

For well over 100 years the **Altnaharra Hotel** has provided countless anglers with Highland hospitality and fishing memories that are today legendary whenever Scottish game fishing is discussed. Resident proprietors Anne and Daniel Tuscher continue that tradition offering access to quality river and loch fishing for salmon, sea trout, and brown trout. The quality of fishing at Altnaharra is reflected in the 1997 returns which totalled 78 salmon, 482 sea trout and 3,167 brown trout.

LOCH NAVER - RIVER MUDALE - LOCH HOPE

Loch Naver enjoys the ability to produce salmon almost from opening day and positive numbers by mid April. Three beats are fished with spinning/trolling permitted in the early season. The **River Mudale** exits Loch Meadie to feed Loch Naver through which it receives it's stock of salmon. It is April before significant numbers of fish reach the hotel beat which includes the famous S bend where the majority of salmon are caught. **LOCH HOPE** among the best sea trout fishing lochs attracts more enquiries than rods available. Fly only is the order of things, with dapped being favoured and reputed to draw the big fish.

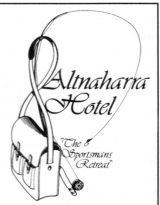

LOCH BORRALAN

Brown Trout & Arctic Char　　　　　**Season 15 March - 6 Oct**

Where the Wester Ross/Sutherland border crosses the A837 about 11/ 2 miles east of Ledmore is one of the best kept angling secrets of the Highlands. **ALTNACEALGACH** is unique in many respects! There's a **REAL Inn**, where you just have room to park between the road and the bothy wall. Right next door (an easy cast away) is a **modern Motel** where first class self catering accommodation overlooks the loch and has a backdrop of Ben More. The loch is up ti' the gunnels with wild broon troot of the 2 to the pound variety that can knock the spots of these peely wally stock pot rainbows in the south, and make a far better breakfast. Any day should produce six to ten brownies with maybe two of 12 to 14oz. The bigger fish are not daft, you have to be good to catch them. However, there are a few taken every season in the 2 to 3lb class. This is a great loch for learning to fly fish with free rising trout taking at almost every cast. Spinning is permitted, maggots are not. The management (Bruce Ward at the Motel) has tagged a few fish which entitles the captor to a bottle of "Scotch". This is a quite unspoiled region great for picnics, hillwalking and ornithology. Quite a few Highland clubs come here for their competitions so it's a good idea to book ahead. The wee Inn is always open, Eric refreshing you at the bar while Christine prepares meals of the home cooked variety till very late. Bank fishing is a paltry £4 per day and there are two boats available at £18 for up to 3 rods. Inchnadamph Hotel also has a boat here. **More details on page 38**

OVERSCAIG LOCHSIDE HOTEL FISHING

Just 16 miles north west of the village of Lairg on the A838 in spectacular Highland scenery the hotel is on the very banks of Loch Shin with bank and boat fishing available. Proprietors Tom and Georgina Gibney will be pleased to answer your inquiries. Tel: (01549) 431 243

other *FISHING SCOTLAND* guides

Inverness-shire - Isle of Skye - Moray & Nairn

Argyll, the Isles, Loch Lomond, Stirling & Trossachs

The ALTNACEALGACH MOTEL

A unique development of new self catering apartments only twenty yards from

Loch Borralan

With free-rising Brown Trout and the best Char fishing in Sutherland Loch Borrolan lies in the magnificent Assynt area of the North West Highlands.

A glance at the map (Ordnance Survey sheet 15) will show you that whether fishing, hillwalking or touring our fully equipped, self-contained apartments are an ideal base from which to cover the whole of this magnificent piscatorial and scenic area.

We are OPEN ALL YEAR so for our current tariff and further information have a chat with the sole proprietors Bruce or Alba Ward

☎ 01854 666 220

The Altnacealgach
by Lairg
Sutherland IV27 4HF
Tel. 01854 666 260

REMOTE? YES!
ONLY A CAST FROM THE SHORES OF LOCH BORRALAN
We do supply the very best of food to:-

Fishermen, hillwalkers, tourists, geologists, ornithologists, potholers, climbers, to lazy self caterers from the Motel next door **AND** we do have a very cosy and comfortable bar where you can relax away from the midges (what midges?) and get in out of the rain (rain?) and enjoy a wide selection of Traditional and Oriental food dishes that will surprise and delight you. A good selection of beers, lager, cider, Guinness on draught, drams and malts will quench your thirst Summer or Winter. Yes, we're OPEN ALL YEAR and ALL day.

FALLS OF SHIN
Visitor Centre Restaurant & Shop
Tel/Fax – 01549 402231

The best place in Northern Scotland to watch wild Atlantic Salmon in their natural habitat. During the season – May to November – salmon jump on the magnificent waterfall as part of their struggle to reach the headwaters to re-start their extraordinary lifecycle over again.

Visit the fine restaurant and shop. Enjoy local food cooked at it's best – including many salmon dishes. Browse amongst the enormous range of goods and gifts in the shop – clothing, foods, cards, books, jewellery, toys, whiskies, wines and fine ice cream.

Let children visit the exciting new activity playground designed to provide interest and thrills for all ages from toddlers to teenagers – and beyond!

There are interesting forest walks from 5 minutes to 1 hour duration. The short walk is designed to accommodate wheelchair access. Dogs are welcome if kept on leads.

Entry to all of the attractions is free.

Open March to October 9.30am to 6.00pm every day.

5 miles from Bonar Bridge   5 miles from Lairg   Follow the roadsigns

WHERE EXCELLENCE COMES NATURALLY

Dunroamin Hotel

has a panoramic view of the river Carron and
Kyle of Sutherland. All rooms ensuite, continental quilts, central heating,
colour TV and tea-making facilities.
Self contained wheelchair access 2 bedroomed flat with
kitchen/lounge & shower room.
We aim at comforts of home combined with excellent cuisine,
including traditional Scottish dishes, vegetarian meals on request,
under the personal supervision of the proprietors.
Packed lunches on request.

Ken & Isabel: Resident Proprietors
Lairg Road, Bonar Bridge, Sutherland * Tel: 01863 766236

Invershin Hotel

Beautifully located on the Kyle of Sutherland!

The hotel has approximately 1/2 a mile of fishing on the Kyle of
Sutherland for brown trout available to guests. Fishing can be
arranged in the river Shin and various lochs and lochans. Write or
phone to establish requirements. All hotel rooms are ensuite with
television and tea making facilities. Full à la carte menu available
and daily home made traditional dishes. Packed lunches available
on request. Freezing facilities available.

Invershin by Lairg Sutherland IV27 4ET Tel: 01549 421202.

PART FOUR
EASTERN SUTHERLAND
DORNOCH & DISTRICT ANGLING ASSOCIATION

This hyper organised association has permit fishing on a selection of lochs and a nice stretch of estuary fishing. Some of these lochs are also available by **Kyle of Sutherland Angling Association** permits. The **Tourist Information Centre Dornoch** with staff always ready to assist with your visitor inquiries issues permits, life jackets and boat keys and accepts fish catch returns. Oh, do not forget to pick up your locally favoured selection of 10 trout flies for only £3.00. With access to such extensive fishings it is a priority that those who's land you enter or cross are accorded due consideration. Please close gates after you pass through, do not light fires, dog must always be under control and leashed and please take your litter with you when you leave a location. Thank you. Popular flies are mainly traditional with Mallard & Claret, Butcher, Blue Zulu, Black Pennel and Kenny's Killer locally favoured in size 8 to 12 dependant on the wave running. Dapping or a big bushy Loch Ordy on the bob brings up the big brownies there is no doubt, so gear up and head for Dornoch. The loch fishing season is 15 March - 6 Oct, except Loch Brora which opens 1 April.

Boat on Loch Brora £15 per day; All other boats £12 per day
Loch bank fishing £5 per rod; Littleferry bank fishing £2 per rod
Lochs Buidh, Cracail Mhor, Laggan and Laro are detailed under the Kyle of Sutherland heading

LOCH BRORA - OS sheet 17 Grid ref 855070
Salmon, Sea Trout and Brown Trout   Season 1 April - 6 Oc
Best known for salmon and sea trout this 3 mile long 3 basin loch carrie a fine head of brownies of the 2/3 to the pound variety with some to 3l taken each season. Though fishing well throughout, the lower easter end has a reputation for consistency. Salmon arrive from spring on wit early May and September most favoured. The larger sea trout arrive i May followed from July on by the shoaling finnock. For the most pa salmon appear to prefer the upper loch while sea trout are take throughout. Warm north westerlies are favoured to produce best cond tions, however, high wind can quickly produce very steep waves and drop in temperature. The south side of the middle loch has rocl outcrops and requires caution as does the narrows between the upp

and middle lochs. Access is direct to the loch side where the boats are kept (near the power pylons) from the Fascally road which exits Brora just north of the river bridge.

XXX BEWARE OF OVERHEAD POWER CABLES XXX

Other sources of boats on Loch Brora are Gordonbush Estate Tel: (0148) 621 323. Rob Wilson Tackle Brora Tel: (01408) 621 373. **The Royal Marine Hotel and The Links Hotel Brora Tel: (01408) 621 252**.

LOCH LANNSAIDH - OS sheet 21 Grid ref 737945
Wild Brown Trout - Rainbow Trout

Regularly stocked with rainbow trout some of which are expected to be in the 2lb plus class by 1996 there is also a high population of native brown trout of 3 to the pound with frequent 3/4lb fish coming to the net. With the exception of a deep pot just out from the boat mooring the majority of this circular wee loch is quite shallow with a pH level of 6.8. Very easy access allows cars directly to the loch side via the Birichen road which exits the A9 about 3/4 mile north of the Evelux junction. Continue on the Birichen road till you top a hill and can see the white Pump station off to your left, the track to the left leads via a locked gate to the Loch. (You will be issued a key with your permit) Boat and bank fishing is permitted.

LOCH LAOIGH - OS SHEET 21 Grid ref 730960

Stocked regularly with hatchery reared brown trout of 3/4 to 11/2lb the average taken is about the 1/2lb mark with a sprinkling up to maybe 21/2lb. Though the banks are mainly of peat the pH level is neutral. Fish are taken from all areas of the loch with the island area a locally favoured spot. The boathouse has a table and chairs should the weather prove adverse to an outdoor picnic. Access is via the Badinish road to the left off the A9 about a mile north of Trentham Hotel. Keep right at all forks till you reach the T junction. The track to the loch is directly opposite between the lay-by and the stream and is only suitable for cars with caution. There is a parking place half way to the loch by the ruined croft or you can go all the way and leave your car on the high ground above the loch, the last 50 metres is boggy.

LITTLE FERRY/LOCH FLEET - OS sheet 21 Grid ref 805955

This is a great place to take family or non fishers for a picnic or a day of nature study. The open landscape of pinewood, sand dunes and estuary with multitudes of dune flowers, butterflies, birds of the pine wood the sea and the waders of the mud flats. A unique summer spectacular are salmon leaping in the sea pool below the bridge while they await the opportunity to move into the river.

From 1 May through 30 September this is a great place to fish for sea trout and finnock additional to the usual flounders, coalfish and mackerel. The bigger sea trout usually appear early in May with finnock from July on. A couple of hours each side of high tide is best . Fishing is from the ruins of the easterly pier eastward to the sea. Spinning is permitted but if you have fly tackle try that - a 2lb sea trout on the fly in the sea is magic. Take the Embo road from Dornoch to the Skelbo Station house. Take the track to the right opposite the Telephone box to the ruins of Little Ferry pier. Beware while wading! There is soft sand and a strong current here.

DORNOCH LOCHANS
RAINBOW FISHING - GOLF RANGE - PITCH & PUTT
Open 10am - 10pm/dusk Mon - Sat - 2pm - 6pm Sunday

Dornoch Lochans has open air recreation in spectacular surrounding for the whole family. The eight stance golf range has a sand bunker and marked target greens up to 250 yards. Hire clubs are available. Pitch and Putt, Croquet and Boules are interesting yet not too competitive family pastimes. The fishing layout is exceptional with 4 lochans fed by natural subterranean source and stocked with best quality rainbows. Two lochs are exclusive to fly fishing with a depth of at least four feet so allowing for all manner of presentation. The rainbow are ideal table fish that average around 11/2lb though the recorded catches indicate fish from 3lb to just over 7lb. Two bait lochs allow the novice the chance to land good sized table fish with hire equipment available if required. The resident proprietor, Malcolm MacGillivray, will be found to be most supportive and helpful and will give you an introductory 2 hour casting session for only £20. The reception cabin dispenses cold drinks, crisps and confectionary additional to hire equipment. Picnic tables and a barbecue stand are located overlooking the lochs with access to the golf range, fishing and toilets designed with the disabled in mind. Altogether at great place or a few hour or day of varied activity and relaxing. Fishing is £2 per hour and fish are charged at £2.10 per pound. 10/20 visit cards and season tickets are available. **Tel: (01862) 810 600** **See advertisement on page 41**

GOLSPIE ANGLING CLUB WATERS

The Golspie club has a method of permit holders becoming club members for only £10 which is reflected in the reduced permit charges to members. After paying membership of £10 the boat charge for up to 3 rods is only £6 on Loch Brora (no bank fishing) and £5 on lochs Buidhe and Horn. Bank fishing is £2 per rod day on Buidhe, Horn and Lundie. On permit purchase a very clear map and description of access together with club regulations is issued.

LOCH BRORA The club has one boats here (no bank fishing) for salmon, sea trout and brown trout. See Loch Brora under Dornoch & D A A section.

LOCH BUIDHE Bank and boat fishing permitted for brown trout. See section on Loch Buidhe under Kyles of Sutherland Angling Association.

LOCH LUNDIE A walk of about a mile is required to this good wild brown trout loch. The wee troot average out at about 2 or 3 to the pound with maybe two in a day being 3/4lb and too big for the frying pan. In a very rural location where you are unlikely to encounter the boom box brigade.

LOCH HORN Within five miles of Golspie there is a steep sharp 1/2 mile climb to this lovely wee loch which due to its position almost always has a breeze to wrinkle the surface. Ready takers here with wee dark flees the order unless mid July has arrived, at which time the Heather moth (Oatmeal) so the best attractor.

Permits issued from Lindsays Store Main Street, Golspie who are open 9am - 1pm and 2pm - 5.30pm Monday through Saturday with early closing at 1pm Wednesday except during July and August.

SUTHERLAND ESTATES HIGHLAND HOLIDAYS

Surrounded by grand Highland aspect with a high degree of privacy these estate homes are renowned for the quality of furnishings and detail of finish. Ben Armine Lodge (salmon fishing on River Blackwater - trout on hill lochs) sleeps 9 and is an exclusive romantic early 19th century hideaway in a beautiful highland setting. Isolated in scenic countryside, Dalreavoch Lodge (salmon fishing on River Brora - trout on hill lochs) is a newly refurbished early Victorian lodge which sleeps 14 overlooking the River Brora. Situated on the shores of The Loch

Fleet Nature Reserve is the Girnal which sleep 10 and was recently refurbished by Laura Ashley. Various fishing is available with house lets including Salmon fishing on the River Brora and brown trout fishing on a variety of hill lochs. Grouse shooting and stalking in season.

RIVER BRORA (LOWER)

Salmon fishing on 4 miles of the lower river is on occasions available for up to 4 rods. A fly only water returns show most consistent figures for late September through August and a steady rise in totals taken with 210 in '94 and 271 in '95 excluding grilse and sea trout. The stretch fished is the south bank from Loch Brora to the Sea with a new fishing hot is erected Ghillie services and casting instruction is under the direction of keeper John Bray. Additionally, there are 7 estate boats on **Loch Brora**, day permit river fishing from Rock pool to the sea, some 3/4 mile of fishing at only £10 a day. Day permits only from Rob Wilson, Brora **Sutherland Estate Holiday Brochure and information available from: Tel: (01408) 633 268**   **See advertisement page 51**

ROB WILSON TACKLE & GUNS - BRORA

This long established tackle shop on Rosslyn Street issues visitor permits for river/estuary fishing and boats on Loch Brora. Estuary fishing is 1 June through 15 October and the loch 1 April to 30 September for brown trout and 15 October for salmon and sea trout. A reliable and experienced river and loch ghillie service is available, with instruction in casting if required . Tel: (01408) 621 373.

THE ROYAL MARINE - THE LINKS HOTEL - BRORA

Famous for golf and highly commended for fine dining these hotels are well able to provide for the angler, a calling in fact they have been quietly following since the year dot. Each season a reserved period on the Brora produces excellent salmon fishing and with hotel boats on Loch Brora that alternative can be quite attractive.

Call **Tel: (01408) 621 252**   **See advertisement page 50**

RIVER HELMSDALE - (Lower) - Fly Only

Salmon and Sea Trout   Season: 11 Jan - 30 September
£15 per day + £2.62 VAT to 1 July then £18 per day + £3.15 VAT
Weekly £70 + £12.25 VAT to 1 July then £90 + £15.75 VAT

This double bank stretch from the head of Flat Pool down to the tail of coach pool is an opportunity to fish one of the most prolific of salmon rivers, not to mention the excellent sea trout fishing which comes into it's own from the end of May on with summer night fishing spectacular. A maximum of 8 rods are available by permit with plenty of room for that number so long as water is in good condition. 4in on the gauge is good for summer grilse and salmon which are at their best from mid June through September. Something in the region of 1 1/2 ft in September will hold the salmon back and provide furious sport in the lower stretches. The day permit is for 24 hours - 9am to 9am which is a wonderful way to permit both day and night fishing. Access is good to all pools. The coach pool is just below and visible from the Bridge Hotel built in 1816 as a coaching Inn, hence the pool name. For permits and reliable local knowledge of the lower river, hill lochs and occasional salmon beats call at: **Strathullie Crafts and Fishing Tackle Dunrobin Street, Helmsdale KW8 6AH Tel: (01431) 821 343.   See advertisement on page 52**

GARVAULT HOTEL FISHING
THE MOST REMOTE HOTEL IN MAINLAND BRITAIN

"You don't get many weeks fishing like that in a lifetime" is a remark that would bring any fisher, meek or intrepid, to a dead stop in their tracks. Well, I can tell you that with diligent research, dedicated fishing expeditions and covert listening in on whispered, winking, head nodding sessions in remote well stocked Highland hostelries such an expression is a reasonable expectation of fishing in this neck of the woods, and its free to Garvault Hotel residents.

The hotel is perched on a wee rise to the north of the B871 overlooking the ancient MacKay's - Sutherland's clan border with Lochs Rimsdale, na Cla'r and Badenloch sparkling in the foreground in Mackay country of open heather and hill as far as the eye can see. Additional to the lochs just mentioned the hotel has fishing on numerious others, some which they control others by arrangement with Badenloch Estate. Many have easy access from the roadside with a walk in of ten minutes to where a day with maybe four to five miles hill walking will allow time to cast on up to half a dozen lochs. The resident proprietors Cath and Tony Henderson, have a finger on the pulse of fisher and outdoor fraternity requirements with good home cooked fayre at the table and packed lunches while the peat fire in the lounge assures you relax and enjoy the banter or nod of dreaming of the morrow.

Bank fishing day permits are £5.00 and boats £15. The bigger lochs really need an engine which you will have to bring with you. May June and September are the most productive months with the warm wester-lies breaking the surface under cloudy skies. Traditional three fly casts and fishing methods are the way to go with dapping from mid summer tempting the big yin's to demonstrate smash and grab tactics. Natives, the troot no less, favour Scottish fayre such as Grouse & Claret, Black Spider, Invica, Loch Ordie, Blae & Black, Dark Mackerel and hairy Heather Moth in size 8 to 10 dependant of the wave. The following are but morsels of this Highland banquet.

GARVAULT - BADENLOCH - AUCHENTOUL HILL LOCHS

The upper Helmsdale loch and run off system is vast, the surrounding area holding more lochs and lochans than days in the year. Days permits for bank fishing can be secured without much trouble however, boats are in great demand as the season progresses with hotels usually the best bet off the cuff. The brief descriptions that follow are just a wee pickle of what is out there. Now use your initiative!

BADENLOCH - Best fishing of this 2 mile long water is from a boat which are kept at the south west corner where you can drive to the waterside. The loch is quite shallow and fishes well throughout though around Rubha Mor Island and the shore and the sandy beach leading to the narrows into nan Clar are particularly consistent as is the area beyond the buoyed skerries off the southern shore. The inhabitants are of about 8 oz. so you can get three in a decent sized frying pan.

LOCH NAN CLAR - A continuation of Badenloch the fishing is similar with numerous 1/2lb brownies to keep you alert. An odd salmon can be expected here from mid season on however with modern cast diameters your 5 or 6 lb cast will be just fine so long as your not to ham fisted. Often described as a dour loch, Bob Beech a long time regular here would dispute that with good reason! But then Bob fishes with some degree of thought fishing the scum lines when there is a real westerly hoolie white capping the waves. Try it, that's where the action is.

LOCH RIMSDALE - As shallow as the others this Badenloch water is 3 miles long and fishes very well all round the shore line by boat or from bank. The lead into and the junction with nan Clar is rocky and requires some care but is a prime provider of heavy trout as is the south west shore particularly when the mayfly makes its appearance. A number of brownies in excess of 3lb are taken each season and as would be expected more than just a few Helmsdale salmon and sea trout fall to the fly on this loch especially when it is dapped in a good wave. Good baskets of breakfast trout are expected with some consistency even with anything less than 2 to the pound being returned.

LOCH AN FHEARNA - Just a big puddle of a 1/2 mile across this is of very easy access with no route march entailed since the Loch Choire Estate road passes within casting distance. A lovely place to drift and cast and come home with plenty of wee fat 1/2lb breakfast troot.

LOCH COIRE NA MANG - Back by Ben Graim north of Auchentoul forest this wee loch requires some little effort of a 40 minute walk in that is all the better for your mental state to attend to detail so you get everything spot on in anticipation of the affray to be staged with one of the Big Fellows who live here and wait for such as you to try pull the wool and tinsel over the other eye. Grand sport here if you have the heart for it.

LOCH ARACHLINIE - Well fed by burn and run off this small shallow loch contains brownies of an average of around the 3/4lb mark with your daily basket containing maybe 2 of 1lb. There are numerous submerged skerries so be aware, however, this is a great bank fishing loch with the shore opposite the boathouse producing excellent sport. A 40 minute walk from Auchentoul Farm will be rewarded with the splendid atmosphere of Sutherland uplands.

LOCH ASCAIG - Here's a wee loch that is just the most ideal place to introduce someone to fly fishing for trout. Located about a mile off the A897 behind Borrobol Lodge. It has good bank fishing with easy no hastle wading.

Some contacts for the above mentioned waters are: **Navidale House, Helmsdale Tel: (01431) 821 258**. Brian Lyall, Kinbrace Tel: (01431) 831 232 has all the right information and contacts. **The Garvault Hotel, by Kinbrace,** call Cath or Tony Tel**: (01431) 831 224**
                                                    See advertisement page 53

STRATHULLIE CRAFTS & TACKLE

Here is a down to earth tackle shop where you will find the that rarity of modern fishing! locally tied flies which look and are of traditional Scottish stock. From wee, wee doubles to substantial spring tubes for salmon. All manner of clothing for all weathers and a very fine gift department where real Highland craft work can be secured for what is always a good price. **See page 53.**

BAYVIEW - BY THE SHORE

Traditional Highland hospitality awaits you in this 19th century traditional cottage on the very shore line not to far from the high tide mark. Ideal for shore fishing and beachcombing. Alistair & Pat Leitch will be pleased to send you full details. **See opposite page.**

NAVIDALE HOUSE HOTEL & SELF CATERING LODGES

Navidale House Hotel has for over a century been a hostelry of some note to salmon and trout anglers. The trout lochs of the area are legend and affording the luxury of fishing at least one new water each day for a week. Navidale's comprehensive trout fishing packages are very popular, so reserve early. **See page 52.**

Garvault Hotel

Props. Tony and Catherine Henderson
Tel: 01431 831224

By KINBRACE – SUTHERLAND

A picturesque house with magnificent views overlooking the lochs. The hotel is fully licensed; comfortable lounges, dining room, pool room. Open peat fires and part central heating make for a relaxed atmosphere. All bedrooms have either private bath/shower.

As well as trout or salmon fishing, the area is famous for its variety of wildlife including birds of prey, red deer, the occasional badger and the fox. Hill walking is an increasingly popular pastime.

"You don't get many weeks fishing like that in a lifetime" is indicative of both the quality of the fishing and the wild grandeur of this remote yet accessible Highland hotel.

READER FEEDBACK/INPUT
FISHING SCOTLAND GUIDES

We feel confident you will find this guide useful and that you will locate some memorable fishing easily while you are in this great Highland region. The services and accommodations mentioned or featured we are sure will be in keeping with the standard professed. We are keen to have your feedback and encourage your input so we can better provide for the visitors of the future. Should you find fishing (which is available by permit) that we have not mentioned, or any detail error in our text, or just want to talk fishin', please write or call any time.

We will be pleased to send each feedback or input letter writer a copy of the next revised edition.

Tight Lines and hast ye' back

James Coutts, 1998.

INCHNADAMPH HOTEL FISHINGS

Season: Trout 15 March - 6 Oct. Salmon Mid May - 15 Oct

LOCH ASSYNT - A good head of brown trout are to be found throughout the loch with ferox (one of 7 1/2lb in 1997) in the deeper cold water which are occasionally caught by those spinning for salmon. Salmon enter the loch via the River Inver and the vast majority of those caught in the loch are taken by the Inchnadamph boats. It is mid June at earliest before any numbers of salmon are present.

TROUT LOCHS - The variety for fishing available is limited only by the anglers choice of distance walked, although one could fish a different loch each day for a week with access by car to the very bank of each. The majority of the lochs hold a high population of Wild native brown trout with an average of a 1/2 lb, while a good day could easily produce a basket with 2 or 3 over the 1lb mark. Indeed, loch trout of 2 to 4lb are regularly on view in the evening when guests present the days catch for considered opinion! Dominated by Ben More Assynt, it would be difficult to find a more majestic setting for a fishing hotel than that of **Inchnadamph.** Situated on the A837 at the south east end of Loch Assynt, Anne Archibald and John Harding continue tradition with a wide selection of fishings for salmon, sea trout and brown trout, all of which are free to guests of the hotel. The charge of £12 per day for boats, £13 for outboard and fuel if required and £1 for life jackets can only be considered nominal by to days standards. With boats on five beats of Loch Assynt, additional to Lochs Leitir Easaidh, Lochborralan, Awe, Ghilaroo and Cam and access to boats on Lochs Veyatie and Urigill guests of the hotel have a rare experience regardless of location. The hotel does not provide fishing on Sundays.

For brochure Tel: (01571) 822202   See advertisement page 63

INVER LODGE HOTEL - LOCHINVER

Perched on high ground overlooking the delightful fishing village of Lochinver, **Inver Lodge** has spectacular views over the Minches towards the distant outline of the Isle of Lewis. Built in 1988, all 20 rooms enjoy the same unforgettable view acclaimed by many guests as the Highlands' finest. The very best of modern comforts is blended with traditional Highland hospitality from the moment one enters the panelled reception lounge, where fishing and stalking trophies provide the atmosphere of a Highland lodge. A Games room provides an alternative to outdoor activity with sauna and solarium facilities to refresh and invigorate always available.

Inver Lodge Hotel controls some of the best brown trout, sea trout and salmon fishing in Sutherland on both loch and river and is the ideal location for that quality fishing excursion where one may hook a 20lb plus salmon on the River Kirkaig, land up to half a dozen salmon from the River Oykel in one day or relish the affray with a 5lb sea trout on the Upper Inver as the golden sun sinks below the evening horizon - When the conditions are right - it's magic.

RIVER INVER (Upper) Per rod day: 5 March - 25 May £20; From 27 May £35; From 1 July - 15 October £70.

Adjacent to the A837 the beat starts at the sluice gates on Loch Assynt down to the burn which enters the river at the west end of 'Battlefield'. Loch Garbh and Loch an Iasgaigh are included with the latter being the best holding pool on the river. The stream from the sluice into Loch Garbh holds fish in high water while the shelf below is good at all water heights. A large head of fish can be resident in Loch an Iasgaich which should be fished from the stream into the neck and down from the hut side first. The water is very clear so stealth, fine casts and small flies are called for.

RIVER KIRKAIG (Lower, Middle and Upper)
Per rod day: 5 April - 29 June £35; 1 July - 15 October £70

The top beat is a good 2 mile walk from the car park and is suitable only for very active walkers such is the elevation of the terrain. Middle beat is not nearly so steep , however, there is a mile long walk to the top pool of this stretch where the proverbial first fish is usually caught. This is excellent water when fresh fish are moving up. Lower beat is very accessible with many of the pools beside the road unfortunately this also attracts tourist to picnic and splash around. Best fished from top down these beats require stealth such is the clarity of the streams and pools.

RIVER KIRKAIG ESTUARY - £12 Per rod day - no surcharge
BENMORE - UPPER OYKEL
Per rod day: Beat One (Top) £70; Beat Two (Lower) £35

The Top Beat is the most productive of the Upper Oykel due mainly to the pools being small, easy to fish and closely grouped together, not least that they are within easy reach from the road. Additionally, the Oykel falls halts fish progress in high water so increasing the resident population below. Light tackle is the way of things for success here with a strong trout rod all that is required. Small dark flies do well with Black Doctor, Stoats Tail, Brown Turkey and Dark Mackerel traditional favourites

Resident guests only may advance book fishing. Trout fishing is free to residents. Non residents Salmon fishing, if available carries £5 surcharge. **For further information contact Nicholas Gorton Tel: (01571) 844496** **See inside back cover for more details**

ASSYNT ANGLING CLUB

With several decades of experience this club is certainly organised in management of 25 lochs of varied potential and size, located over a wide region of hill and mountain terrain stretching from Ardroe on the north west coast above Lochinver to the western slopes of Quinag above Loch Assynt Lodge. Divided into 4 groups, the main one is located to the north of the main A837, requires minimal walking and is the most popular. There are 2 lochs here with boats, however the real pleasure is in walking from loch to loch enjoying the wilderness feelings of casting to catch wild brown trout. The second group are wee lochs on the Ardroe peninsula where the size of the lochan has no direct bearing on the size of the native inhabitants. This enlightenment has frequently been brought home to late for the angler with tackle too fine for the job of containing wild broon troot which from 2 or 3 to the pound to whatever! Only by going out there, casting a fly and being quick enough to respond will you ever really know. South of Inverkirkaig the 'Cat' and 'Dog' lochs both have boats, are of easy access with the road running between them. 'Jewel in the Crown' undoubtedly is the group of **Lochs Cam** (20), **Veyatie** (21) and **Fionn** (22) which can be accessed from Kirkaig, however, to walk in from Elphin is much easier. Energetic and able walking is required for those last mentioned lochs. Go, do not put it off, the spectacular scenery with miles of bank fishing will live with you forever. You need Ordinance Survey map sheet 5 and the ability to read it. Additionally, common sense dictates Stout boots or shoes, wind and waterproof outers and food to last longer than your plan could be an inspired move. Midge repellent or a face net will add to your pleasure and some Wee dark flies with a heather moth or two if

August has arrived will help to provide the breakfast. Do not light fires, dogs are prohibited from hill country and please take all you litter off the hill with you. The club supplies a good diagram of the loch locations with your permit purchase. Permits from Tourist Information Centre; Simpsons Newsagent; Ardglas Guest House; The Fish Selling Co, Lochinver; Highland Stoneware, Ullapool; Tourist Information Centre, Lairg. Cost: £6 per day for lochs 20, 21 and 22, all others are £5 per day; £25 per week; £50 per two weeks. Boats are available only from A. Munro, Ardglas Tel: (01571) 844 257 who also conducts fly casting instruction.

ASSYNT CROFTERS TRUST

History was made in 1993 when a group of over one hundred Crofters set out on the first Crofting Community Buy Out of their land. This truly beautiful wilderness is just laden with hundreds of freshwater lochs and puddles, some with fine reputation for Wild trout, some of unknown potential. These lochs are a valuable resource of the Crofters Trust and by buying permits and completing return records you will be contributing to the long term development of this land. The lochs lie in the region known as North Assynt Estate, which is the area from Stroer Point east to a border running from Loch Nedd south west to Tuirk Loch, to the Manse Loch and so to Loch Roe just south of Achmelvich. (*** FLY ONLY**)

LOCH CROCACH * The ideal learning experience! Just bursting with wee troot urgent to tug at any reasonably cast fly.

LOCH CUL FRAIOCH * The deep pink flesh with a delicious flavour has both local and visitor returning in spite of blank days to ply another design in the hope of landing one or two of these unique wild brownies.

LOCH DRUMBEG * With a long-standing reputation for high quality fish it is little wonder the popularity. In beautiful environment the two boats here are seldom on the shore. Calum Millar, The School House Drumbeg. Tel: 833 269 can provide casting instruction.

LOCH na CLAISE * A boat is available here from McKenzies in Stoer Tel: 855 226.

LOCH POLL The largest of the lochs contains Char, with runs of sea trout and salmon. The brown trout are prolific with many heavy fish being caught each season. The Loch Roe, Manse and Tuirk system has a good run of sea trout when there is a freshet from May on.

The Trust issues a detailed map of the lochs with permits which are obtainable from: Stoer and Drumbeg Post Offices; The Tourist Information Centre in Lochinver; Simpson's Newsagent, Lochinver; Day £5; Weekly £20; Two Weeks £30; School children £2.50 per day £5 per week. Boats: £10 per day plus permit fee.

PROTECTION ORDER 1994 NO. 3302 (S.194) IN EFFECT
KYLESKU HOTEL

Surrounded by the breathtaking scenery of Quinag, Ben Mor Assynt, dramatic sea views and splendid glens, rivers and lochs the KYLESKU is an oasis in the wild wilderness of western Sutherland where the hill walker, ornithologist, geologist and fisher will find unspoiled participation with the environment. The hotel is modern with west Highland hospitality always evident. Marcel Klein, the resident proprietor provides also the expertise of Chef with extensive experience in Europe and a delight of sea foods and local west Highland produce including venison, lobster, scallops and salmon. The hotel has arranged some exceptional wild brown trout fishing on the North Lochinver and Reay estates which is complimentary to resident guests. **For brochure please call Marcel. Tel: (01971) 502 231.   See advertisement on page 63**

SCOURIE & DISTRICT ANGLING CLUB

This club leases **FLY ONLY** fishing rights of 33 lochs in the region north of Scourie village, bounded by the A894 Scourie to Laxford Road . The lochs are well posted by a board with the loch identification number. Any loch not known to contain trout is not marked on the very excellent map provided with permit purchase. Some of the lochs require little walking while the most remote provide the bonus of a walk in Highland wilderness and all that goes with it. The club has several boats which are available for hire. Fishing is not permitted on Sundays. Permits are issued from 9am daily Monday through Saturday from: Mr & Mrs H. Mackay 12 Park Terrace. Scourie (The end house opposite the shop) **Day rod - £4; Week (6 days) £16; Boat per day £4; Day Rod hire £4**

SCOURIE HOTEL FISHING

This long standing and well known fishing hotel has boats for salmon and sea trout fishing on Loch Stack in addition to access to over 250 lochs and lochans on the Reay Forest Estate and Kylestrome Estate. Residents of the hotel fish without charge with the exception of Loch

Stack where guests are additionally required to have a ghillie at the daily rate of £35. With such large areas of mountain and glen the walking distance to lochs can be anything from a short walk to several miles in the course of a days fishing. Some latitude would be expected with the catch! The more isolated the loch the more likely you are to strike trout of exceptional proportions. For further details Tel: (01971) 502 423

REAY FOREST ESTATE

This large sporting estate is situated in the remote and ruggedly beautiful North West Sutherland with Self-catering cottages available within a few miles of Achfary village on the A838 Lairg to Laxford Bridge road 30 miles west of Lairg. The area is of great attraction to walkers, geologists, ornithologists and botanists additional to the wonderful fishing possibilities of Lochs Stack, More and the hundreds of hill lochs many of which have boats. Loch Stack and More - The headwaters of the Laxford River, have long provided attraction for anglers to return again and again to continue the saga of exceptional sea trout and to a lesser extent salmon. Boats are available at £27 per day for 2 rods while hill loch fishing is charged at £3 to £5. For further details of cottages and fishing: Reay Estate Office, Achfary, by Lairg. Tel: (01971) 500221

RHICONICH HOTEL

With sea views from the head of Loch Inchard , the hotel retains fishing on at least 11 brown trout lochs and the River Rhiconich which together with Loch Garbet Beag provides alternative sea trout and salmon fishing within the 11,500 acre estate. Eight boats are located on a variety of trout lochs providing a splendid and diverse choice of waters most of which are reached with only a short walk. Fly Only is the order of the day with permits issued from the hotel on a day or weekly basis. The salmon season is 11 February to 15 October and the brown trout season 15 March to 6 October. There is no Sunday fishing. Tel: (01971) 521 224.

Gyrodactylus salaris; A Threat to Salmon
Alasdair H McVicar, FRS Marine Laboratory, Victoria Road, Aberdeen.

Gyrodactylus salaris (GS) is a small skin fluke, but the effects of this parasite on salmon populations in a river can be devastating. In western Norway, salmon have disappeared from almost 40 rivers within about two years of the infection first appearing in them. The same would probably happen in Scotland if the parasite was introduced here and steps have had to be taken to avoid such a catastrophe.

GS infects the skin of Atlantic salmon, Arctic charr and rainbow trout and appears to be naturally present on salmon in the rivers of the eastern Baltic Sea, with little damage to their skin. The Baltic stock of salmon are not seriously affected by GS infection. In contrast, salmon stocks from outside the Baltic do not have any resistance to the infection and all infected fish probably die due to heavy infections and severe skin damage.

GS has a natural constraint to its spread as it can not survive in full strength sea water, but from around the mid 1970s the parasite appeared for the first time in rivers in western Norway. New occurrences have been recorded almost every year since. Proof is still lacking of the actual cause of spread of the parasite, but the transportation of live salmon parr and rainbow trout for restocking, fishing and fish farming purposes remains high on the suspicion list. GS has now also been shown to be present in rainbow trout in several other European countries but to be absent from the UK. Strict legislative control on the import of live salmonids to the UK since the 1930s has been a major factor in avoiding the disease. In the 1980s, GS was made a notifiable disease to afford more protection. At the instigation of the UK, further safeguards were introduced in 1996 when the EC granted special protective measures to the UK by restricting imports of live salmonids to areas where the parasite has been proven to be absent. Currently, Ireland is the only Member State which can meet the requirements and move live fish to the UK.

As the parasite can survive for a short period away from fish if kept cool and damp, materials such as fishing equipment, which have recently been in close contact with infected fish and waters are also a potential risk. To inform anglers and fishery owners of this risk a pamphlet outlining the problem and suggesting appropriate practical steps which could be taken has now been distributed widely.

- Only anglers who have recently been fishing abroad are a potential risk. If fishing here within a week of returning, they may choose to use local equipment.
- Equipment (boots tackle) can be made safe by drying at room temperatures, by prolonged immersion in hot water (such as in a bath) or by freezing.
- If none of the above safeguards is achievable, one of several chemicals may be used (such as are employed before equipment is used in some other countries).

Further information can be obtained from the above address.

Discover the secrets of Sutherland
from the comfort of

The Kinlochbervie Hotel has a fine reputation for its food and wine. Overlooking the village and lochs with panoramic views to the open sea. Each of fourteen bedrooms has en-suite bathroom, colour TV, radio, telephone and tea or coffee facilities.

After a day of fishing, walking the unspoiled coastline or just contemplating the 'quality of life' nothing quite compares with the anticipation of the evening's dinner menu of fresh seafood direct from the harbour, hill lamb and venison of quality served with dedicated experience in the dining room overlooking the bay.

................A trip worth making.

FISHING for wild brown trout in the many lochs on nearby Estates. Sea trout and salmon in the famous Sandwood Loch itself. Tight control of permits issued in conjunction with the John Muir Trust ensures the solitary fisher can be just that!

SEA FISHING on quality marks can be arranged for parties of up to twelve. Big cod, haddock, hake, skate and bass abound in these waters.

SHORE FISHING our local guide will show you the best spots all very much under exploited with specimen cod, pollack, and hard fighting bass in season waiting to test your skills.

HILL WALKING & CLIMBING the choice is endless for the Munro Bagger or the Easy Rambler. A wide choice of walks and climbs are available to guests with helpful maps and route details provided as part of the service.

DIVING in our clear waters is an unforgettable experience. We can organise trips for up to twelve to explore seas, caves and wrecks along the coast. Our service includes bottle refilling, cleaning and drying facilities.

BIRD WATCHING our late spring and summer trips to sea bird colonies are not to be missed by ornithologists. Sea trips to otherwise inaccessible areas are carefully controlled to ensure maximum enjoyment for guests and minimum disturbance for the birds.

For further details contact: Linda McHattie, Resident Manager
KINLOCHBERVIE HOTEL
KINLOCHBERVIE BY LAIRG – SUTHERLAND – SCOTLAND – IV27 4RP
TEL: (01971) 521 275 FAX: (01971) 521 438

KINLOCHBERVIE HOTEL FISHING

The fishings in this area embrace all three game specie in waters that vary enormously in size and character. There are half a dozen sizeable lochs, numerous hill lochs, one good burn and a smaller river that hotel guests may variously access. The country is wild and utterly unspoiled, yet the fishing waters are easily accessible. Most of the lochs have been little fished for many years with less than proper analysis of the fishing or returns. Brown trout run up to 2lb or more though the majority of native inhabitants are of the 3/4 lb variety. There is both river and loch salmon and sea trout fishing which by nature requires a good freshet to encourage these fish from the sea. All *FLY ONLY,* the following is typical of Kinlochbervie fishing.

LOCH INNIS NA BA' BUIDHE This medium sized loch just behind the hotel is in a low ground valley with a short outlet to the sea which allows sea trout and occasional salmon and grilse to enter any time from July through August with the right conditions. A normally early loch, May and June are best when brownies of 3/4 lb are the norm. Though access is easy bank fishing is quite rough going in places, so take care.

LOCH NA LARCH A small shallow loch on flat ground with easy access from the road just a mile north of the hotel. Bank fishing is good and easy with brown trout of better than average up to 2lb. Again May and June best unless it has been a very cold spring.

LOCHAIN NAN SAC A wee loch with bigger trout which are difficult to catch. Dour is the local expression, however, if two or three trout a day of up to 1 1/2 lb each is the kind of fishing you are chasing this is the place! Situated in a heathery hollow with a 1/2 mile walk.

LOCH SANDWOOD At sea level and separated from the sea by a wide sand bank this loch is fed by the River Shinary the target of sea trout and salmon that enter the loch. Some excellent brown trouting which comes on in late April. Permits are very limited.

The Kinlochbervie Hotel, where residents enjoy some free fishing, can provide quality bank and traditional boat fishing for a limited number of anglers in superb Highland surroundings where the preservation of quiet ambiance and natures process is paramount. Day permits are from £5.00. Private, family or small group **"Learn to Fish"** trout fly casting excursions, including equipment, can be scheduled for residents.

DURNESS LOCHS - CAPE WRATH HOTEL FISHINGS

The lochs out on west side of the Kyle of Durness are the mecca for the angler who likes solitude and the ability to walk and fish perhaps 3 or 4 typical Highland lochs in a day without so much as the sight of another fisher. A ferry boat will take you across the Kyle or you can leg it in from the south. It is however the 4 limestone lochs of Keoldale, that attract the inspired anglers who have fished here previously or read of exceptional sport. The clear water and shy nature of the inhabitants demand patience and fortitude in addition to ability if one is to produce the desired results. Dependant on conditions both dry and wet fly can produce equal attention. **Loch Borralie** is the largest just a short walk from the hotel and produces 3 to 4lb trout with surprising regularity, as does the others of the group. **Loch Caladail,** a little smaller is most accessible and provides sport equal to the other waters. **Loch Lanlish** is the smallest loch and is very popular with a record return showing many fish in excess of 5lb. **Loch Croispol** appears to provide smaller fish with more consistency than the others yet still manages to kick that out with fish of 4lb plus. Further details and permits are available from: **Cape Wrath Hotel, Durness. Tel: (01971) 511 212. See advertisement page 70**

TONGUE DISTRICT ANGLING CLUB

Strung round either side of the Kyle of Tongue the fishings consist of 8 brown trout lochs available by day permit. Additionally, there is sea trout fishing with Spinning permitted only on the Kyle. The lochs are of easy access with those off the road still easy walking for all but the infirm. Club permits are issued at Ben Loyal Hotel & Tongue Hotel.

TONGUE HOTEL

A former Victorian hunting lodge built in 1880 the hotel stands on a hillside overlooking the golden beaches of the Kyle providing select accommodation and traditional Scottish Fayre with warm Highland hospitality. The hotel has secured some fine 2 rod beat salmon fishing on the River Borgie for May through September 1998. The first fish of 1998 came of the Borgie in mid January so by normal standards there should be a good head of salmon in the river from mid May on. There is excellent brown trout loch and sea trout fishing locally additional to club water permits avialable at the hotel. For the non fishing this is spectacular Highland country. **See advertisement page 69.**

BORGIE LODGE HOTEL FISHINGS

The 'Royal' antlers and the greens and reds of the Sutherland tartan which greet you at the entrance hall convey the way of things to come at **Borgie Lodge**.

The hotel has 20 hill lochs listed and ready for a cast that range from large roadside waters with boats to remote (10 to 30 minutes walk) lochans where massive water creatures in the garb of trout have put the fear o' death in unsuspecting anglers in search of just a wee troot for breakfast. **LOCH LOYAL.** Situated with easy access from the A836 this large loch is fishable from either boat or bank. A good place to learn to fly fish with many small fish of 2 or 3 to the pound clambering for the fly. Occasional salmon are taken - now that's another story. **RIVER BORGIE.** This fly only river drains Loch Loyal and tributaries to run 6 miles through rugged peatland then beautiful Borgie forest to the sea at Torrisdale Bay which it shares with the River Naver. The best months for salmon are March, April and September with a fine run of grilse expected through June and July. The first salmon off the river in 98' was taken by Jim Stewart the water bailiff on the 21 January, a nice 11 lbr. Access is very good and is via a forest road which parallels the river. Little wading is required with a 10 to 11ft sea trout rod the ideal instrument. With only 4 beats of 2 rods and 3 day rods there are more than enough pools to keep one occupied. **Day rods cost £20 each. 2 rod beats are £375 to £475 plus VAT per week.** At the head of the River Borgie **LOCH SLAIM** enjoys a heavy grilse run from May through June to add spice to the excellent wild brown trout which average 3/4lb. Exclusive to the **Borgie Lodge** a 20 minute walk is required with only one boat available, no bank fishing. The surroundings are just magic while the ability to spin or worm fish allows for all contingencies. **Day permit £20 inclusive.** Peter and Jacqui MacGregor the proprietors, fishers themselves, enjoy as much as you the tension of the stealth cast, the explosive enthusiasm of the solid take and the contentions of the play. You, however, will benefit from their experience and expertise in arranging the nitty gritty stuff so you just play the lady or laird in just surroundings. Well go on, call right now.. **Peter and Jacqui are at Tel/Fax: (01641) 521 332**

See their advertisement on page 70

RIVER NAVER - ASSOCIATION WATER

This stretch of the famous river has 3 very good pools and 3 excellent sea trout runs from the road bridge upstream to the head of Ally's pool, 300 meters long and holds a head of fish from June on. Day permits (3 only) can be purchased the day prior to or the day of fishing only from the **Tourist Information Centre** Bettyhill. Though fish are taken from mid January it is mid May before any number show with June and July the most productive. The first fish of 98' were grassed on the 21 of January. No doubt, this is first class value with like returns.

Permits: 3 available daily - valid 6 am - 9pm - £14 each

RIVER NAVER - ESTUARY BEAT

From the road bridge downstream to the sea the River Naver estuary beat produces many fine sea trout and salmon each season with no charge effected to the angler. The no cost water opens into a beautiful sandy estuary with rock and sand banks from which one can spin or fly fish. Fishing is great in the spring with many heavy fish (5 to 8lb sea trout) being grassed or sanded as the case may be. This is an excellent gesture by the proprietors providing some little attraction for anglers to tarry in this remote village a wee while longer. Enjoy.

MELVICH HOTEL

Overlooking the estuary of the River Halladale on the Pentland Firth the hotel is ideally situated and convenient for fishing the Halladale the Naver (just twelve miles west) or the numerous brown trout lochs in Strath Halladale. For the 1998 season the Martin's have an in house brewery providing REAL ALE for those inclined to such fine manner of thirst quenching.   **See advertisement opposite.**

RIVER HALLADALE

The lower Halladale is 8 miles of river divided into 4 double bank beats carrying 3 rods per beat. All beats are of easy access for all age groups, are provided with comfortable huts and rod racks while most pools can be fished without wading. The Upper river is 3 miles of double bank fishing with a further 3 rods. Storage reservoirs upstream provide some degree of additional freshet and inducement for fish to run. Further inquiries to: Strath Halladale Partnership. Administration Secretary Miss A. Imlach. Tel: (01641) 571 271

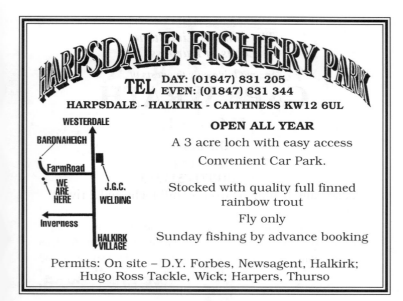

HARPSDALE FISHERY PARK

TEL DAY: (01847) 831 205
EVEN: (01847) 831 344

HARPSDALE - HALKIRK - CAITHNESS KW12 6UL

WESTERDALE
BARDNAHEIGH
FarmRoad
WE ARE HERE
J.G.C. WELDING
Inverness
HALKIRK VILLAGE

OPEN ALL YEAR

A 3 acre loch with easy access
Convenient Car Park.

Stocked with quality full finned
rainbow trout
Fly only
Sunday fishing by advance booking

Permits: On site – D.Y. Forbes, Newsagent, Halkirk;
Hugo Ross Tackle, Wick; Harpers, Thurso

CAITHNESS'S FIRST PUT & TAKE FISHERY
OPEN ALL YEAR – HARPSDALE – FLY ONLY

Situated about two miles south of Halkirk it's on the left with a good farm road leading to the car park just to the left of the farm house. About 2 1/2 acres when opened in mid 97' the plan is to extend by about another acre for the 1998 season. Access is very easy over grass directly from the car park (about a minute and a half if you stroll) and there should be picnic tables and a wee shelter by late spring 98'.

Stocked with brown, brook and rainbow trout to 8lb. it's the writers guess that there will be high demand for the limited permits issued.. **Sunday permits** must be booked at least one day in advance.

Permits are £6.00 X 2 hrs. (1 fish); £11.50 X 4hrs. (2 fish); £19.50 X up to 7 1/2 hrs. (4 fish). A season ticket with a catch limit of 35 fish is £140.00. Single lures are permitted (no pellet flies, boobies or wrigglers) Wet or dry multi fly casts are permitted.

Permits are available at the park, at **D. Y. Forbes, Newsagent, Halkirk, Harpers Fly Fishing Services, Thurso. Tel: (01847) 893 179 & Hugo Ross Fishing Tackle, Wick. Tel: (01955) 604 200.**

Fishing in Caithness!
There's just one stop!
Permits! Tackle! Clothing!
Boats!

We <u>are</u> fishing!

HUGO ROSS
56 High Street, Wick
KW1 4BP
Telephone: (01955) 604200
Fax: (01955) 604200

PART SIX
CAITHNESS

Unspoilt, beautiful and peaceful are expressions both first time and frequent visitors use to describe the "John O'Groat Peninsula". A 700 square-mile triangle of inland rolling heather moor and spectacular coastline bordered to the south and west by rugged mountains. In the interior the 'Flow Country' is a vast watery wilderness covering hundreds of square miles relieved only by the seemingly endless groups of trout lochs and rivers. Bird and plant life abound attracting naturalists and ornithologists. Flat and fertile, the north eastern corner was known as the bread-basket of the Viking empire which today contains fine farming land surrounding exceptional trout lochs. Rich in archeological sites with long-cairns from 5,000 years ago, Bronze and iron age structures and much evidence of Viking attentions provides interest and insight to history. Entering Caithness from the south, one passes the cliff villages of Berridale, Dunbeath and Latheron to travel 'Over the Ord' a headland and deep ravine the major barrier to access until very recently. Dunbeath, birthplace of Neil M. Gunn Author of 'Highland River' and 'Silver Darlings' has a Heritage Centre of note, an excellent introduction to Caithness. There are **Tourist Information Centres at Wick, Thurso and John O'Groats.**

The **Dunbeath Hotel Tel: (01593) 731 208** an old coaching Inn dating from 1830 is quietly situated in the village just off the A9 with sea views and easy access to a multitude of trout lochs. For brochure contact Pat and Neil Buchanan the resident proprietors. **See page 76**

Latheronwheel Estate, situated some 17 miles south of wick, makes brown trout fishing available on Lochs Ruard, Stemster and Rangag which are accessed from the A895 with but a short walk to Rangag and Stemster while Rhuard is a good 45 minute hill hike and not available after 12 August. Bank fishing is £3 per rod and boats £12 per day. Lochs are Fly Only and produce trout of the 1/2lb variety in considerable numbers. For permits and information call the Keeper, J. Anderson Tel: (01593) 741 230 or **Hugo Ross Tackle - Wick Tel: (01955) 604 200.**

Thrumster Estate has permit Fly Only trout fishing on the 4 lochs Hempriggs, Scarclet, Yarrow, and Brickigoe which lie almost by the roadside from 3 miles south of Wick. Yarrows 'Marl Loch' appendage is well known for heavy trout which are hard to catch! With such easy access and 1/2lb average trout these are popular evening fishing lochs in summer. Most productive months are June through September. Bank permits are £4 per day with a season ticket at £25 and £12.50 for juniors. Boats cost £12 per day or £6 for evening or half day from Thrumster Garage or **Hugo Ross Tackle - Wick.** **See advertisement page 72**

HUGO ROSS FISHING TACKLE - WICK Tel: (01955) 604 200
Centrally situated at 56 High Street the **Hugo Ross** store has been extended in floor size and is well able to meet the anglers and outdoor enthusiasts every need including camping equipment, outdoor clothing, maps, a fine book selection and all the flies, lures and tackle you will require for successful fishing in the highlands. Hugo and his staff have extensive practical local experience and offer an enthusiastic welcome to the visitor. Open 9am to 5.30 pm Monday through Saturday permits are issued for: **Lochs Watten, St. John, Toftingall, Calder** all of which have boats with a private lunch hut at Watten and Toftingall. Hugo also issues permits for the **River Wester,** the **River Wick** association water and can on occasions come up with a day or two of private beat salmon fishing. **See advertisement page 72**

WICK ANGLING ASSOCIATION WATERS
RIVER WICK - Salmon & Sea Trout   Season: 11 Feb - 21 Oct
ALL FISH MUST BE RETURNED FROM SEP. 30.
Except in times of spate this is quite a slow moving narrow river with a fall of only 1 ft for each of the 10 miles from Watten to the sea. However, with between 300 and 400 salmon grassed most seasons and a good number of heavy sea trout. Double bank access is easy at most of the 40 named pools with no wading required, and association huts located at pools 25, 29 and 35 on the excellent location map produced by Hugo Ross. Locally favoured spots include the Strath above Haster, about 3 miles upstream where the many bends with pools tend to be the first resident stretch, the pot at Watten mill and Flag Pool right behind Loch Watten Hotel. Salmon are expected from late March with summer rain giving the best prospects and conditions when heavy grilse runs add to the action. Spinning is permitted till 15 May and worm fishing from 1 May through 30 September. Handlining the fly is on occasions required due to the slow moving water and the need to induce action to

the fly. Size 8 and 10 Ally's Shrimp, Stoats Tails, Munro Killers and Hairy Mary are tops with Toby spoons and silver Bridun Mepps the popular spinners. **Permits: £10 per day, £37.50 per week till 1 May then £20 and £70 respectively thereafter. Evening permits are available for fishing 5pm till dusk at £10 per rod. From: Hugo Ross Fishing tackle. High Street, Wick.**

RIVER & LOCH OF WESTER - Salmon & Sea Trout

Permit fishing is available on both of these waters which produce vast numbers of sea trout and a few salmon. Just 6 miles north of Wick off the A9 a season ticket is just £40 with a 50% discount for senior citizens and juniors. 5 to 7 visitor day bank permits which cover both river and loch are available at £10 each with a 2/3 rod boat costing £10. Permits and bookings from: **Hugo Ross fishing tackle, Wick.**

LOCH WATTEN - Brown Trout - Season: 1 May - 30 September

Below the crystal clear waters of Watten the limestone, marl and protecting weed together provide the conditions of first class trout habitat which gave this loch the reputation so badly dented in the early 90's when abuse reduced past quality of fishing. The loch requires some degree of patient fortitude and is not for the fickle! Is however, a good place for beginners who require some such experience early in the game. The silvery trout with pink flesh reflect ultra fertile feeding to average around 3/4lb with a good day providing maybe 2 at or over the 1lb mark so it would appear that the loch is on the mend! Any improvement should be evidenced in the next few seasons. A well tried local fly cast is Black Pennel, Soldier Palmer and Peter Ross with a Loch Leven Spider early and late in the season if the breeze is chilly. No Dogs or fires are permitted. Bank fishing permits cost £2 per day and £6 per week (No Sunday Fishing) Boats at around £15 from dawn till dusk are available from: **Harpers Fly Fishing Services, Thurso (01847) 893 179; D. Gunn, Estate Office (01955) 621 217; Hugo Ross Tackle - Wick (01955) 604 200** has a private pier, lunch hut and picnic area at the north west end accessed from the A882. The Loch Watten hotel is presently closed however, Just 16 miles from the loch in Thurso the **St. Clair Hotel Tel: (01847) 893 730** offers packed lunches and late meals to anglers as does the **St. Clair Arms Castletown Tel: (01847) 821656.**

ST JOHN'S LOCH IMPROVEMENT ASSOCIATION

Dedicated management and fortitude in resolve by this association have resulted in water which deserves its position as THE premier loch of the county. Situated in the neck of the Dunnet Head peninsula the loch is fished by boat or from the south shore which is actually a very productive alternative to drifting a boat. Such is the close to the sea location it is rare to find no breeze to break the surface, the opposite however, can create white caps and quite steep waves. Additional to traditional boats the association has a 'Wheely' available (only from Harpers, Thurso) which works in well with the facilities of the Castle Arms Hotel just 4 miles east on the A836 which provides a wheelchair access chalet.

The season opens the first Saturday of April and closes 30 September. Stocked for 20 years now with indigenous fish from the association hatchery the pink fleshed average is 3/4lb which is confirmed by returns. For about three weeks from Mid June prolific Mayfly hatches provide the kind of sport that has duffers believe they have arrived in the promised land with 2lb trout alternately straining line and the anglers heart. This is a definite "must fish" loch which requires prebooking in high season. **Bank permits: £3 per day, £2 an evening, boats £12 for 2 rods per day or £6 an evening. Float tubes are £8.00 per day & £4.00 per evening. No Sunday fishing.** Permits and boats from: Northern Sand Hotel, Dunnet; Castle Arms Hotel, Mey**; Harpers of Thurso; Hugo Ross of Wick.**

DUNNET HEAD LOCHS - This group of small lochs scattered around the headland area produces the usual 2 or 3 to the pound trout with a few exceptions which take some stalking. A nice area with easy access for a family picnic. Permits from Dunnet Head Tea Room, Brough. Harper Fly Fishing, Thurso. £10 per week, £3 per day.

HARPER'S FLY FISHING SERVICES - THURSO

Just bursting with stock to cover all manner of sea and freshwater fishing, outdoor clothing, boots, camping gear and Government surplus **Harper's** is located at **57 High Street** adjacent to the car park. The Proprietor Graham Brooks and his staff are experienced local fishers and well able to advise and assist accordingly. Open daily Monday through Saturday bank and boat permits are available for: **River Thurso - trout; Loch Calder** (Sunday Fishing)**; Loch Heilen; Loch Scarmclate; Loch St. John** (boat hire, including a wheely)**; Reay Lochs** (Sunday Fishing)**;** Occasional fishing may be available on private beats and fly casting instruction can be arranged to include rental equipment if required. **Tel: (01847) 893 179**

See advertisement page 77

RIVER THURSO - ULBSTER ARMS HOTEL

Salmon , Sea Trout   Season: 11 January - 5 October

With 13 rotating beats each with up to 10 productive pools the 25 miles of river from Loch More to the sea provides more than ample space for the allocated rods. Beat 1 is used by the Thurso Angling Club while all others are let by the week. With fish taken in March in the upper river there is little doubt that salmon indeed run in January and February although serious fishing does not get under way until March. April and May see a steady rise in fish caught with June holding steady before the summer runs of both Salmon and grilse in July take off through August and September. There are some quite slow sections of the Thurso where handlining and backing up are a tradition which produces excellent results and requires only a little practise under the eye of an experienced ghillie, certainly not the mystic claptrap frequently professed. Good water level is as always paramount and the effect of Loch More is to extend the period the river fishes well without rainfall. Tube flies from 2 to 3in are used most in the cold spring weather with doubles and long shanked trebles of 8 to 10 size in Hairy Mary, Munro Killer, Stoat's Tail and Ally's Shrimp all in fashion these days.

THE TROUT LOCHS

The are 12 trout lochs of some repute the most remote of which require walks of around 2 miles with the remainder of easy access from roads as are the 3 streams available. The better wild native trout stocked lochs show an average of 9 to 12oz over 2 years with individual fish to 2lb no surprise. All fisheries are Fly only, traditional 3 fly wet casts being fished from a boat. Soldier Palmer, Zulu, Coch y-Bonddu and Black Pennel provide ample response. For more details contact: **Estate Office, Thurso East, Thurso, Caithness. Tel: (01847) 893 134 or The Manager, Ulbster Arms Hotel, Tel: (01847) 831 641.**

See advertisement page 77

RIVER THURSO - THURSO ANGLING ASSOCIATION

The association has day permit salmon and sea trout fishing available for the Lower and Upper sections of beat 1 where visitors are welcome. The season is 11 January - 5 October with an unspecified and varying charge throughout the season. No advance booking is permitted, day Permits as available are issued daily by **Bike & Camping. High Street, Thurso**.

LOCH CALDER

Just five miles south of Thurso this partly spring fed loch has good bank and boat fishing over marl, sandstone and shingle with some peaty water along the west shore which fishes best from a boat. The eastern shoreline has nice wee bays and promontories, all good trout water where bank fishing takes as good as boats of the frisky two to the pound inhabitants with maybe a couple heavier fellows up to two pounds on a reasonable day. The location is such that there is almost always some breeze to assist in the great fly deception. Bank permits are £3 a day and boats £15 from: **Harpers of Thurso or Hugo Ross in Wick.**

LOCH TOFTINGALL

A long narrow loch treed mostly to the shore. A private gated road leads to the boathouse on the western shore. I have fished this marl and sandstone loch frequently in recent years, only from a boat and enjoyed it every time. The trout are solid fighters and must average out close to one pound. Traditional Highland flies have stood me in good stead here with my usual Invicta, Soldier Palmer and Dark Mackerel always providing a good meal, of trout. The evenings can be calm but I found a dry Heather Moth or Greenwells tempted well. Boats are £15 a day and bank permits £5 from: **Hugo Ross of Wick**.

REAY LOCHS

Limited traditional fly fishing on good quality secluded brown trout lochs, guided excursions, casting instruction and equipment by arrangement, for individuals or small groups. Day permits £5 or £10 the week. For Information contact: Lesley Crawford Tel/Fax (01847) 811 470 or **Harpers Fly Fishing Services. Thurso Tel: (01847) 893 179.**